HOMES ARE FOR PEOPLE

HOMES ARE FOR PEOPLE

Satenig S. St.Marie

John Wiley & Sons, Inc.,
New York London Sydney Toronto

Library of Congress Cataloging in Publication Data:

St. Marie, Satenig.
  Homes are for people.

  Includes bibliographies.
    1. Interior decoration—Psychological aspects.
I. Title.
NK2113.S25   747'.01'9   72-10244
ISBN 0-471-82635-9

Printed in the United States of America

10 9 8 7 6 5

This book has been mulling in my mind for a long time. It is not intended to be a "how-to" book in the sense of teaching the basic technical and design considerations in furnishing a home. This has already been done, and done well, by many authors before me.

It is, rather, a philosophical statement about home and its importance in shaping human lives, because this aspect of home furnishing has not been explored fully enough by educators, writers, or researchers. There is so much more that we all must learn about the impact of the home environment on the development of the creative soul within each human being.

I have tried to apply research about human needs to practical applications for the planning of furnishings for the home, using many illustrations as sources of ideas instead of as definite solutions to solving interior design problems. Hopefully, they will spark the creative thinking of the individuals who use this book.

It is my firm belief that a home planned to focus on the psychological and sociological needs of people can make a significant contribution to mankind. An unknown Chinese poet wrote:

I carved a willow branch
 The wind brought me the sound of a distant flute.

Who is to say that a home furnished to meet human needs isn't the significant factor that will influence the sound of that distant flute?

Satenig St. Marie

To my dear husband
Gerald
whose patience and encouragement
and yes, prodding, too
on days when I didn't feel like writing,
made this book a reality!

Writing this book has been both a rewarding experience and a frustrating one. It was satisfying because I had something to say and when the words flowed easily, it was nourishment for the soul. But it was a long hard task, too, and at times it seemed like an albatross hanging round my neck.

To the many friends and professional peers who have been so supportive during the years this book has been in process, I want to express my heartfelt thanks. Although they are not mentioned here individually, I will not forget the important role each played. They shared the burden of the albatross and it helped!

Some persons made unique contributions which must be acknowledged separately.

☐ Dr. Beatrice Paolucci of Michigan State University counseled and advised, brought important concepts to my attention, and reacted to sections of the book as they were written. Words are inadequate to express my appreciation to her.

☐ Esther Warner, author of *Art: An Everyday Experience* inspired me with her African Fable about man and the home he created. I appreciate the permission to reprint it in this book.

☐ Mrs. Chieko Akiyama from Tokyo, Japan, made it possible for me to visit the homes of three of her friends in Tokyo and to learn from them how Japanese families relate to their home environment. It was an experience I will always cherish.

☐ Darlene McGovern, my secretary, advised and reacted to the manuscript from the point of view of youth. Her comments influenced the direction of many chapters.

☐ Miss Beatrice Billings, a dear friend of many years sent me a wealth of information about homes and families in the Orient and the South Pacific based on her experiences in working there. Her insights were most helpful.

This acknowledgment would not be complete if I did not thank the many companies and individuals who so generously gave me pictures to use with the manuscript. The pictures have done so much to expand the concepts and I hope they will be the spark to light the imagination of all who use this book.

Satenig S. St.Marie is Director of Consumer Affairs for the J.C. Penney Company, Inc.

Her interest in teaching home furnishings to meet human needs began when she was a County Extension Home Economist working with families in Connecticut and Massachusetts to help them plan meaningful home environments. Her graduate work included studies in art and home furnishings, both in New York and in Europe.

Mrs. St.Marie was elected to be President of the American Home Economics Association for 1973–1974. She is also a member of AID and the National Home Fashions League, Inc.

She holds a B.S. degree in home economics from Simmons College, Boston, and an M.A. in home and family life education, with a minor in art and home furnishings from Columbia University.

Mrs. St.Marie is listed in *Who's Who of American Women, Foremost Women in Communications,* and *Two Thousand Women of Achievement.*

Contents

HOMES ARE FOR PEOPLE

INTRODUCTION

An African Fable: The Beginning of Wisdom

The beginning of wisdom,* says a West African proverb, is to get you a roof.

Here is the West African folk tale from which the proverb is taken:

When Maker had finished fashioning the first man out of a scrap of clay, Maker set man down on the crest of a rainbow and gave him a small push which sent him sliding down to earth over smooth, fire-bright color through thread-soft rain. When man finished this grand slide through the sky, he stood upright and looked upon the new earth to which he had come. Man felt fear. He looked back up the bright band of color and longed to return to Maker. The long curve of the rainbow was slick and steep. There were no hand-holds to help the climb. Man made a few determined tries. He could not rise one step. There was no return.

Man turned his back on the sky-bow and sat down with his head in his hands. His body shivered in the rain. His heart was cold. Man was lonely. Lonely is cold.

Maker, standing at the top of the rainbow, looked down on the shivering loneliness below and was sad. "I should not have sent man down there," Maker thought. "But it is done. Well, at least, I'll send down after him a packet of Sense. That will help a little."

Maker wrapped Sense in a scrap of cloud and sent it down the rainbow after miserable man. The packet hit man in the middle of the back with a thump.

Man jumped to his feet and clutched Sense to his heart. The Sense in the packet was this:

1

"All the good in the world is home-spawned. The bad in the world can not find you under a roof of your own. Go, now! Get you a house."

Man pulled the cloud-wrapping from the Sense packet around his shoulders and had his first length of cloth. He began walking over the earth to which he had come, wondering how to get him a house. Rain-soaked mud oozed between his toes. The mud weighted his feet. He stepped up to a patch of moss on higher ground and raked at the mud with a fallen stick. When he cleaned the twig with his hands, he saw that the shape of his hand stayed in the clay, that the clay took form from his strength.

"Of these things you can make you a house," Sense told him. "Of sticks and this mud that stays on the stick and takes shape from the strength of your hands, of these you can make you a house."

When the house was built of a circle of sticks with mud forced between them, and only a door-hole was open, man went inside. He felt he had grown. He had a larger feel than when he had huddled at the foot of the sky-bow. But even with walls, he shivered because the house had no roof and the rain continued to fall.

Man looked up and saw fronds of palm trees above his head. He saw that the rain was stopped where the leaves were thick, that at the center of the tree the trunk was dry.

"Bring many leaves close together," Sense whispered. "Then you will be dry and warm."

Man roofed his house with palm thatch and saw that he had done a fine thing. He felt large; he felt warm. He was not so lonely now because lonely is cold. He was not so small now, because large is the feeling from making,

from making the earth take form from the strength in the hands.

Man was hungry when this much work was done and went out of his house to find himself food. He came to a pool and saw that fish swam there with the colors of the sky-bow on their backs.

"I will have fish," man thought, and reached for them with his hands. Man fell in the pool and "lacked small" to drown. Swim-knowing was not part of the Sense packet wrapped in torn cloud. Man could have died then and never have slept in his new house except that a turtle saw him sinking and showed him what he must do to swim.

"I thank you plenty," man said when he was safe. "What, now, can I do for you?"

"Throw me a scrap of Sense, I beg you," Turtle said. "Maker never gave me a packet of Sense."

Man told turtle how he must build him a house and have a roof of his own where the bad of the world cannot reach.

Man, knowing how to swim now, caught fish while Turtle built a roof over his back. When Turtle was finished, Man saw that Turtle had done a one-more-again thing. There was pattern over the whole! Man took pleasure in what Turtle had done.

"How will I pattern my house?" Man thought about this all the way home.

When Man stood before his own walls and once again cleaned the mud from his feet with a stick, the thing he might do became a knowing in his hand. He was tired but he could not rest until he had made a pattern, much like Turtle's, by scratching his walls with the stick.

"I am clothed with a cloud, I am fed by a fish, I am roofed by leaves, and now I will take rest," Man thought. He stretched out on the floor of his house and listened to the rain drum on his roof. The sound was good. He wished Turtle had come home with him so they could listen together to the good sound that rain makes on a roof. He thought over his first day on earth. "A stick is a hand-thing." With the damp stick clutched in his fist to give comfort, he slept.

Food, clothing, shelter, were necessities but so was the "one-more-again thing!" Man's house became home with that. It was not an extra. It was not "art." It was a need. It had to be done before Man could take rest.

Man had discovered the beginning of wisdom—he had created a roof that was more than a shelter—it was a home, his home.

He had felt the need to be creative, to experience some kind of environmental mastery. Erich Fromm describes it as the need to feel the creator, to transcend the passive role of being created; to express individuality.*

This book is dedicated to helping individuals and families become aware of the importance of home not only as a major force in helping man to express individuality, but as a force that can make a significant difference in meeting the truest human needs.

* Erich Fromm, *The Art of Living*, New York, Basic Books, Inc., 1963, p. 43.

FURNISHING
HOMES
FOR
PEOPLE

The role of home as an environment for human growth is a significant one. It has the potential to support human life in a meaningful way, influencing the development and behavior of individuals and families and improving their quality of life.

So often, however, home seems to become a stage set according to rules and cliches, instead of an environment planned to help individuals grow and develop to their fullest potential.

What makes the difference? And how does one develop the know-how to create an environment to which individuals can relate? The task is not an easy one. It takes a lot of understanding and insight into human needs; and it is a challenge to some of the traditional concepts about planning the interior of homes.

Perhaps, the place to start is with human needs.

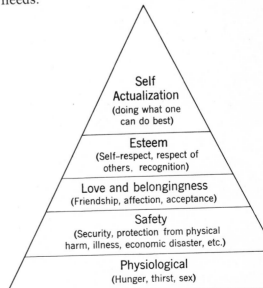

Self Actualization
(doing what one can do best)

Esteem
(Self-respect, respect of others, recognition)

Love and belongingness
(Friendship, affection, acceptance)

Safety
(Security, protection from physical harm, illness, economic disaster, etc.)

Physiological
(Hunger, thirst, sex)

According to Maslow, human behavior is motivated by a desire for satisfaction of several different kinds of needs, from the most demanding (physical) to the highest and most ultimate (self actualization). Some take precedence over others. Further, if a number of an individual's needs are unsatisfied at any given time, satisfaction of the most demanding ones will be more pressing. In order of precedence, they are shown on the preceding page.

Once the lower needs are fulfilled to some degree, then the next level begins to emerge; "gratification of one basic need opens consciousness to domination by another 'higher' need." Hence, the gratification of one's physical and safety needs can lead to an awareness of the need for love and belongingness; the gratification of this level can lead to the need for esteem and, finally, to the need for self-actualization—the need to be what one is capable of being.

Usually, all levels of needs exist in people to some extent most of the time. The need for food (hunger) need not be fully satisfied for the needs of safety, love, esteem, and self-actualization also to be present. Each individual interprets his needs according to his own culture, tastes, values, feelings, family, attitude about self, job, and money.

Maslow describes self-actualization thus:

"Even if all these needs . . . (the lower level needs) . . . are satisfied, we may still often (if not always) expect that a new discontent and restlessness will soon develop, unless the individual is doing what he is fitted for. A musician must make music, an artist must paint, a poet must write, if he is to be ultimately at peace with himself. What a man can be, he must be. This need we may call self-actualization."

" . . . the human being has within him a pressure (among other pressures) toward unity of personality, toward spontaneous expressiveness, toward full individuality and identity, toward seeing the truth rather than being blind, toward being creative, toward being good, and a lot else. That is, the human being is so constructed that he presses toward what most people would call good values; toward serenity, kindness, courage, knowledge, honesty, love, unselfishness, and goodness."

To what degree home influences an individual's interpretation of his needs will depend, of course, on the individual situation. The potential for positive experiences is obvious, both for each person and for the family as a unit. Space and activities for the most demanding needs are usually considered essential, even in the most traditional homes. It is the *less tangible needs* in the hierarchy that must be thoughtfully considered when planning the home environment. For example, family activities in the home can meet different needs of different individuals at the same time. Consider a family birthday party:

For the Mother. She may be fulfilling her need for being creative, which may be one of her means of self-actualization.

For the Family. It may provide a feeling of love and belongingness while fulfilling the need for food.

For the Family Member Honored. The party may meet the needs of recognition and esteem.

Opportunities for sharing responsibilities and decisions by all family members, at the level of their capabilities can help meet these intangible needs, too. Certainly, decisions related to home furnishings and space allocation are one way to achieve this. Planned times for the family to be together, such as mealtimes with a pleasant, relaxing atmosphere, and family rituals for holidays, are another.

Not to be overlooked in all this, are the physical aspects of the house. An environment that requires care and upkeep beyond the time and energy capabilities of the occupants can leave little time for the really important needs of people.

Besides Maslow's hierarchy, other human factors also must be considered in planning home.

Creativity is one. As already stated in the prologue, Erich Fromm has pointed out that man has a basic need to be creative, to express his individuality. This need was a relatively easy one for home to fulfill in days gone by when it was necessary for each family to produce its own foods and household supplies. There was plenty of opportunity for all family members to be creative and involved. Today, technological advances have streamlined this procedure, and people must find other opportunities for creativity. Furthermore, standardization in all aspects of living today presents a real challenge to this innate need in man. Consider the uniformity created by mass production of prefabricated houses, or the owners of apartments who make endless rules about what families living in their facilities can and cannot do.

The problems that can be created when man cannot meet his need to be creative are described by Mathew Dumont:

"We must learn that the environment is responsive to us, that some part of the cosmos, however small, yields to our touch, is beckoned by our will or is shaped by our hand. If we do not learn this at all, we carry the burden of a severe emotional disability. If we learn it inadequately or out of scale, we may have difficulty in mastering our own impulses or we may become preoccupied with the will to power, a need to control others that will dominate our lives as well as the lives of our victims. If we do learn this lesson well and in proper scale and then are thrust into the environment which is no longer responsive to us, we become enraged. . . . The need to feel some control over the environment, to leave a fleeting imprint of one's foot or hand or soul on the matrix of the world is a basic psychological need and the frustration of that need can wreak havoc."

Here, then is another human need that a thoughtfully planned home must provide opportunities for individuals to fulfill. It may be in small ways like involving family members in decisions about selection or placement of furnishings; it could be situations that are planned so that individuals have opportunities for self-expression—in space planned for hobbies, in assigned responsibilities and chores that carry authority as well as responsibility,—in an area of the home each can call his own.

Stimulation and overstimulation are another set of psychological factors that home can do something about. Psychiatrists are learning that where there is an insufficient ratio of adults to children, there seems to be a deficiency in the intellectual and emotional adaptability of the children. Children deprived of the stimulation of parental figures cannot develop to the fullest. Conversely, it has been suggested that children who need to spend a great deal of their time in the streets because there isn't enough space for them inside the home can become overactive because of too much stimulation, and this can lead to delinquency, theft, and other behavior problems learned as a result of constant roaming through the community. In one respect, then, home can be a refuge from overstimulation.

In another respect, home can provide variety and sensory stimulation. Psychologists are now finding that a monotonous environment, which deprives the senses of stimulation, can be harmful to mental health. The brain needs sensory intake and stimulation for optimum development just as the body needs food for growth.

Endless jokes have been made about women rearranging furniture, but maybe one of the reasons some homemakers rearrange furniture in the home frequently or change the curtains and slip covers seasonally is an unconscious recognition of this need for variety in the environment.

Perhaps one of the most far-reaching effects of home is the role it can play in helping individuals develop a value system, to have the opportunity to find out what's important. Sorting and clarifying values is a life-long process that man must pursue if he is to make his life meaningful and his self complete.

The family, of course, is very important here. Paul Lemkau defines a healthy family as "one in which unity of aim and purpose has been worked out by the partners and which has created habitual ways (rituals) for symbolizing these aims, which when observed, give the family individuality of which it is con-

scious enough, so that it can grant the right of individuality to the children raised in it. Such a family would have enough energy left over to contribute to the creative individuality of the larger social sphere, relations with neighbors in the community and in larger social or government groupings."

A healthy family builds a sense of family solidarity through shared experiences and activities, opportunities for dialogues between all members, and the setting for learning how to form bonds with other human beings. Home for the family then becomes a place to learn skills, and to watch adults at work; it also becomes the place to teach cultural behavior, where sensitivity and creativity can be encouraged, individual needs recognized and nourished; where happy memories are made, and where love builds security and self-confidence. Sentimental? Maybe. But isn't the emotional side of life important, too, and isn't the family home a logical place to learn how to trust and use our emotions as well as our minds — to develop our humanity?

In today's fast paced world, where everyone seems to be on a treadmill, home and family can be the oasis where individuals learn to develop inner resources and search for meaningful values and goals, where they build a personal philosophy and have time to look at the whole high world with wonder.

Besides influencing the needs of people, the family as a major socialization force in the home also influences their growth. Its position is rather like an acrobat walking a tightrope. Our earliest and most fundamental values develop when we are children in the family circle and from close relationships and contacts who are admired and respected. As a child grows and begins to experience the world around him, both through mass media and the outside world, if values outside the home are different from those held by the family (which may be a different cultural, ethnic, or economic group), he may have difficulty sorting out feelings and loyalties. It becomes imperative, then, that the family be aware of changes in society, reflect these changes, and try to adapt to them in the home, without losing its identity or its cultural heritage. The last is especially important, since any part of a culture which adds meaning and value to the lives of the individuals in the family is significant. It becomes a matter of constantly sorting values to keep in tune with the times, and to preserve that which is meaningful to the unique situation.

In pioneering days, the family was responsible for religious, educational and recreational functions. Today, outside forces have assumed many of them.

The changing role of the family has made it a mediating function, a buffer between the individual and society. Externally, it must adapt to social and industrial changes of institutions in society while, internally it must adjust to the needs of individual family members. For example, consider these familiar situations:

The World of Work. Some jobs have night hours, some daytime hours, some require work on Saturdays and Sundays. The family must adjust its living pattern accordingly. Some companies transfer employees to different locations in this country and even to other countries; or, the breadwinner may wish to change jobs and get a new one in another community or even another state. "Collectively and individually, family members uproot themselves, adapt to a new city or

neighborhood, enter different schools, make new friends."

The only stabilizing factor may be the home environment with its familiar surroundings.

The World of Education. The educational system may require parental supervision of homework, money for daily lunch, may pressure parents to be active in PTA, and may set double shifts, imposing time and money adaptations on the part of the family.

The Inflexibility of Time. Schools, churches, and places of work set time schedules. The family must adjust. These institutions in the interests of serving the most people with efficiency can become cold and impersonal. Class must start on time, trains must run on schedule, and production lines must not be held up.

The family has to adapt to these outside forces and still be flexible enough to provide the emotional balance individuals need, the forgiveness if one is a few minutes late, the understanding if mistakes are made. Only a small unit such as the family can provide this flexibility.

With the rapid technological strides being made, the family situation in the home, with its adaptive function, may well be a key in socializing individuals to the flexibility needed to live in a rapidly changing society.

Perhaps an extra word or two is appropriate at this point on the concept of the family. There are some in our society who say it is changing. That the familiar nuclear family—mother, father, and children, living in a common household, with the father as breadwinner and mother as full-time homemaker is not a psychologically rewarding situation. Furthermore, others point out that we are leaving many other kinds of living situations out when we think only in terms of the nuclear family. For example, the one-parent family, the three generational family, the dual-work family, the couple without children, middle aged and old couples and even cluster families which have been described by Herbert Otto as "a circle of three to five families with generally similar aims, goals and values, meeting regularly and sharing specific family functions and services. Each family maintains its own home as a base."

The increase in the number of working mothers is also changing the complexion of the nuclear family.

Whatever form it takes, and we will surely see more life styles emerging as viable alternatives in the future, the family, in its broadest concept needs to provide a climate in which human beings can flourish. It may even need to be the force that stands up to so many of the changes that society is forcing on the family, and begin to demand that society make some adaptions to suit the family.

Regardless of the form of the family, the home, as an environment for housing it can be carefully planned to teach flexibility and adaptability when it is needed to keep pace with society's changes, while also encouraging the human assets of man — love, beauty, sensitivity, morality, ethics, the clarification of values, and the building of a philosophy of life.

With these thoughts in mind, furnishing a home takes on new significance. It is no longer a matter of "rules" to learn about where to hang pictures, or what colors to combine but, instead, becomes a significant experience to create an environment in which people live, both as individuals and as members of a family, — an environment meaningful in human terms that can influence each individual to grow and develop to his fullest potential, since only as each individual reaches self-actualization can he be a force in improving society and the world around him.

SOURCES OF INFORMATION

Bettleheim, Bruno, "Design: The Human Dimension." Professor, Psychology and Psychiatry Director, Orthogenic School, University of Chicago, Chicago, Ill. (Comments made at NEOCON)

Downer, Donna Beth, Smith, Ruth H., and Lynch, Mildred T., "Values and Housing — A New Dimension," *Journal of Home Economics*, Vol. 60, No. 3, March 1968.

Geiken, Karen F., "Expectations Concerning Husband-Wife Responsibilities in the Home," *Journal of Marriage and the Family*, August 1964, pp. 349–351.

Hook, Nancy C., and Paolucci, Beatrice, "The Family as an Ecosystem," *Journal of Home Economics*, Vol. 62, No. 5, May 1970, pp. 315–318.

Hurd, Helen, "Mid Pleasures and Palaces" Penney's *Fashions and Fabrics*, Fall and Winter, 1964.

Kyrk, Hazel, *The Family in the American Economy*, Chicago, Ill., 1953.

Lee, Dorothy, "Home Economics in a Changing World" Penney's *Fashions and Fabrics*, Spring and Summer 1964.

Lemkau, Paul V., M.D., "A Psychiatrist's View of Housing," Proceedings: Seventh Conference for the Improvement of the

Teaching of Housing in Home Economics Land-Grant Colleges and State Universities, October 30 to November 2, 1963. College of Home Economics Publication No. 180, Pennsylvania State University, University Park, Pennsylvania, 1964.

Luckey, Eleanore B., and Wise, George W., *Human Growth and the Family*, Graded Press, 1970.

McArthur, Arthur, "Developmental Tasks and Parent-Adolescent Conflict," *Marriage and Family Living*, Vol. XXIV, No. 2, May 1962.

McCullough, K. P., Smith, R. H., Wood, A. L., and Woolrich, A., "Space Standards for Household Activities," Bulletin 686, University of Illinois Agricultural Experiment Station.

Man in a Changing Environment — New Concepts of Time, Beauty, Space, and Social Relations. Proceedings of a one-day institute sponsored by the New York State College of Home Economics, at Cornell University, April 18, 1967.

Maslow, Abraham, *Motivation and Personality*, New York, Harper & Brothers, 1954.

Maslow, Abraham (ed.), *New Knowledge in Human Values*, New York, Harper & Row, 1959.

Montgomery, James E., "Impact of Housing Patterns on Marital Interaction," *The Family Coordinator*, July 1970, pp. 267–274.

"What is Self Actualization?" Penney's *Forum*, Fall and Winter 1969.

"Values," Penney's *Forum*, Fall and Winter 1968.

Thomas, Walter L., "Values and American Youth," *Journal of Home Economics*, Vol. 61, No. 10, December 1969, pp. 748–754.

Vincent, Clark E., "Family Spongia: The Adaptive Function," Presidential Address presented at the Annual Meeting of the National Council on Family Relations in Toronto, Ontario, Canada, October 1965.

Warner, Esther S., *Art: An Everyday Experience*, Harper & Row, New York, 1963.

THE
NEED FOR
PERSONAL
SPACE

Whether planning the furnishings for an entire home, or the logistics of a given activity in the home (such as a party) people are involved in a basic problem: the use of a given area of space. A relatively new science, proxemics, is providing fascinating insights into man's psychological needs for space.

According to Dr. Edward Hall, professor of anthropology, Northwestern University, individuals use and experience space in everything from interpersonal relations to the architecture of the buildings in which they live and work. Furthermore, each person has around him an invisible bubble of space that expands and contracts according to what he is doing at the moment, and his position in each given social situation (for example, whether he is in a leadership position, a guest, or a member of a group). It is also influenced by his cultural background and his emotional state.

This invisible bubble is always with the individual. Others seldom are permitted to penetrate it, and if they do, it may be for only limited periods of time.

Many outside forces can change this bubble and can create discomfort for the individual. A crowded or cramped area created by architecture or the arrangement of space in a room which places strangers or remote relations in close proximity can create feelings of aggression toward others. And if an individual is already in an emotionally tense state (this may have been the day something went wrong at home or at work!) the sense of distress about cramped space may be even more acute.

Just imagine a crowded waiting room in a bus terminal, or a small home or apartment that must be shared by two or three families, or a bedroom that must be shared by too many individuals, without enough space for activity or storage of possessions. These types of situations which crush or dent man's space bubble can create as much damage as though his body were crushed. The only difference is that the effects may not be as evident as quickly.

And, in contrast, a space that is compartmentalized and seals off an individual, removing him from human contact, can create just as aggressive a feeling.

How does an individual know when his space bubble is being disturbed? Space is perceived by all the senses, and each sense makes its own contribution to the perception of space. Auditory space is perceived with the ears, thermal space with the skin, kinesthetic space with the muscles, and olfactory space with the nose. Therefore, space overcrowding is caused as much by overstimulation of the senses—too much noise, too much undesired physical contact, too much thermal heat, too many odors—as it is by the physical limitation of space.

Consider the following:

How do you feel when you sit in a chair recently vacated by someone else when you can still feel their body heat on the chair?

Has the noise from a neighbor's party, TV set, or barking dogs ever annoyed you?

What happens when too many relatives come to visit and stay for an extended period of time, causing crowded living conditions in the home?

What is your reaction to the smell of burned food? Cigarette smoke? Perfume?

What kinds of feelings do you experience when you are bumped in a crowded bus, train, or subway?

How do you feel on a bus, train, or plane if there are children crying continually?

Recent studies have revealed the influence of space on animals as well as people. In one study, social and physical pathology doubled when room size (square meters per inhabitant) fell below a certain critical limit. Another study found that animals repeatedly stressed by overcrowding developed alarming symptoms as well as deviation from normal behavior.

Of course, overcrowding of space bubbles cannot be measured by one situation or one set of circumstances. It can build up during the course of the day. For example, a ride to work or school on a crowded bus or train, a day of work in an office shared with many other persons, or lessons in a crowded schoolroom, lunch in a busy cafeteria and the return home via crowded transportation can all create stress. It can be relieved in part by the buildings that house individuals.

According to Dr. Hall, a building can act as a screen or a container. If home is planned as a meaningful environment for people, it can act as a screen to reduce overstimulation of the senses from crowding by the outside world. Public buildings, on the other hand, are usually containers that are planned for the work that needs to be done, instead of for the space needs of individuals. As these buildings become overcrowded, the stress on individuals increases.

It is of interest at this point to observe that the population increase in this country has created more crowded homes. Therefore, each generation has less and less space in which to live.

In the 1800's, the Victorian houses had large rooms with high ceilings. There was ample space in which to live. The thick walls and high ceilings provided accoustical isola-

14

The feeling of space is very evident in this New York City Victorian Drawing Room. The high ceiling and ample dimensions of the room minimize constraints on individual bubbles.
(Photograph by Byron, The Byron Collection, Museum of the City of New York)

15

In contrast to the spacious Victorian room, this contemporary living room seems small. However, with careful planning it has been made to seem more spacious. To begin with, a wall of windows carries the eye beyond the four walls to the garden outside. Then, there is a feeling of unity created by the rectangular lines of the furniture which repeat the lines of the windows.

tion and conveyed a feeling of privacy. The homes were large enough so that each family member had space to carry out his daily activities. Today's homes, in contrast, almost force constant togetherness because they are more compact, ceilings are lower, rooms are smaller, and they are not always suited to the needs of family members.

The challenge, therefore, to make the existing space work for human needs should be one of the basic concerns of home furnishings. The amount of space an individual requires in part depends on whether he is a contact person or a noncontact person; and this depends on his cultural background. Generally speaking, "contact" persons come from the following cultural backgrounds:

> Italian, French, Spanish
> Russian, and Middle European

Noncontact persons are from these backgrounds:

> English, German, Belgium,
> Scandinavian, Swiss, and Dutch

How does this apply to furnishing a home?

Contact persons might want these space arrangements:

A large kitchen where several people can work together at once, or where more than one activity can be carried on at one time.

A bedroom used by two where shared activities are encouraged.

Chairs in an area close enough where they can "touch" the person they are talking with in conversation.

A noncontact person would want:

A small kitchen that excludes other persons from working there at the same time, or a large enough kitchen where activity areas

16

The furnishings in the room are less elaborate than those in the Victorian room and are smaller in scale so that the overall proportion is in keeping with the space in the room.

(BURLINGTON HOUSE AWARD WINNER submitted by Margery Phillips of the Seattle Times)

are separate and there is ample space around each so more than one person can work without coming in contact with the other.

A shared room with definite divisions of areas for use by each individual.

A tiny room for a place to study so that there is space for no more than one to work at a time.

If a "contact" person marries a "noncontact" person, these cultural differences that influence space must be considered so that each has satisfactory living space somewhere in the home.

Have you ever stopped to think about your own reaction to space needs?

When you walk into a room or an office, do you sit in the chair nearest or furthest from the other person?

Do you automatically pull your chair closer as conversation gets underway, or do you push your chair back, indicating that your space bubble is being penetrated?

Have you ever felt that some rooms were closing in on you?

How do you feel if someone sits very close to you and continuously touches you during a conversation?

Dr. Hall has found that the amount of space during conversation influences the level of voices of those involved.

Very close (3 to 6 inches)—soft whisper; top secret.

Close (8 to 12 inches)—article whisper; very confidential.

Near (12 to 20 inches)—indoors, soft voice; outdoors, full voice; confidential.

Neutral (20 to 35 inches)—soft voice, low volume; personal subject matter.

Sometimes a tiny room is ideal for a noncontact person, especially if there's room for only one person to function efficiently.
The arrangement of desk and chair in this compact study define the work area, and can easily screen the space bubble of the individual working at the desk since there isn't room for another chair to be placed nearby. (1971 BURLINGTON HOUSE AWARD WINNER submitted by Martha J. Walters of The Nantucket Inquirer-Mirror)

Neutral ($4\frac{1}{2}$ to 5 feet) — full voice, information of nonpersonal matter.

Public distance ($5\frac{1}{2}$ to 8 feet) — full voice with slight overloudness; public information for others to hear.

Across the room (8 to 20 feet) — loud voice; talking to a group.

Stretching the limits of distance — 20 to 24 feet indoors up to 100 feet, outdoors; hailing distance, departures.

Each individual has his own unique way of filling space and of using space for daily living. Each cherishes his space and wants to defend it from outsiders.

Think about:

Who traditionally sits at the head of the table where the family eats?

What happens if someone sits in a seat you were using when you get up to leave the room and return again to find "your seat" taken? How do you feel? Are you annoyed because they took your seat?

What about certain territories in the home that are associated with individuals:

☐ Dad's chair. He always sits in it to read the paper or watch TV, and if anyone else sits there, they are sitting in "dad's chair," and may even feel they need to apologize to him and get up to give him his chair if he should come into the room.

☐ The family pet's favorite spot.

☐ The homemaker's kitchen.

☐ A man's study or workshop.

☐ "My" room or wishing for a room of one's own.

With all this in mind, the planning and use of space in the home emerges as a major force in molding man. Home must provide the privacy needed to smooth out the "dents" made in the bubbles during the day; it must be planned to allow enough space for the needs of individual family members, to screen the family from the stimulation and stress of the outside world. Also, it must be flexible enough to respond to changing needs: to provide privacy when needed and to bring people together when desired.

Defining and Shaping Space. Once an understanding of man's basic space needs is recognized, the problem becomes one of applying this knowledge to defining and shaping space in the home.

How it is done will depend on two variables. First, the needs of the individual family must be clearly understood. Is it a contact or noncontact family? Does it need screening from the outside world? How many individual space bubbles must be considered? How many outsiders visit in the home and how often? Then, after the human needs are determined, the available space can be analyzed. If there is not enough space ideally for all needs, priorities will have to be set. Perhaps there will have to be a series of "trade offs", with some space needs being cut in order to provide adequate room for others. Ideally, when such "trade offs" are to be decided, input from all family members concerned should make the choices easier to accept.

Organizing the space itself can be done in many ways. The following illustrations are examples of some individual approaches to defining and shaping space.

Some Approaches to Defining Space.

This space is visually shaped by unifying the windows and wall area with colorful laminated shades and a matching cornice. With the chair and desk in the same colors as the shades, the area, visually, becomes one space.

(Courtesy Window Shade Manufacturers Association)

Sometimes the design of furniture pieces shapes space, as this bed unit that separates the area for rest from the area for play. This arrangement would be quite suitable for "contact" rather than "noncontact" children, since the space is defined by functional areas rather than personal area.

(Courtesy Wallcovering Industry Bureau and American Enka Carpet Fibers)

A creative young couple shape space in this large room by use of a plywood section, painted a bright color, which gives the impression of a private area for rest by forming a floor to ceiling headboard for the bed. A cut out at the top holds a bright Mexican piñata, contributes to a feeling of spaciousness to this apartment.
(1971 BURLINGTON HOUSE AWARD WINNER Photo Courtesy of Glamour © 1970 Conde Nast Publications)

A large kitchen like this one may work equally well for a contact or noncontact person. For the former, there's plenty of room for family and friends to visit or help. For the latter, there are enough clearly defined work areas so that physical contact with another person will not be necessary and he can keep his space bubble undisturbed.
(Courtesy of Kitchens by Coppes-Napanee, Nappanee, Indiana)

See-through furnishings, whether they are in the form of
plastics, or slender legs on furniture, psychologically fill
less space in a room because they don't block out large
areas. Thus, a relatively small room will not seem to be
quite so crowded.
(Courtesy J.C. Penney Company, Inc.)

25

One very obvious way to have a spacious area is to use a minimum of furniture. That's just what was done by a bachelor in Chicago who got rid of everything in his cluttered apartment and started all over again. This is the living-dining room in his studio. Not shown is a trunk used for storage of wines, and a neon sculpture. (1971 BURLINGTON HOUSE AWARD WINNER sub-mitted by Susan Root of The Chicago Daily News)

*The shape of the furniture in relation to the shape of the
room can also be a factor in creating a feeling of space.
The large rounded chair echos the rounded lines of the
fireplace wall. The same feeling of lines is repeated in
the design of the Rya rug on the wall. A sparsely
furnished area, planned with sensitivity to form and
texture becomes quite spacious.
(1971 BURLINGTON HOUSE AWARD WINNER "Unusual Dwelling in the Southwest")*

A stairway separates the living area from the dining and
food preparation areas on the next level in this home.
Because all areas are visible to the eye at one time, the
space appears larger than it really is.
(1971 BURLINGTON HOUSE AWARD WINNER submitted by Kay Elliott of The Washington Evening Star)

Skylights always add a lively feeling to space. These are equipped with translucent shades installed from bottom up to permit control of light when desired. The placement of the furniture along the walls leaves the center of the room open for a feeling of more space. (Courtesy Window Shade Manufacturers Association)

A very simple yet functional window treatment can provide for privacy and still extend the feeling of space in a room. Here, two sets of shades, one hung slightly below the other, are designed to function independently. The transparent fiberglass shades protect against bright light without blocking out the view. The outer shades can act as room darkeners when needed. Both harmonize with the horizontal lines of the seating and storage unit on the opposite wall.
(Courtesy Window Shade Manufacturers Association)

A high ceiling, not very often a part of today's homes, definitely gives a room a feeling of space, and the personal air bubbles plenty of room to function!! This interesting room is a week-end retreat on the shore. The lofty chimney of the black iron stove-fireplace also carries the eye up.
(1971 BURLINGTON HOUSE AWARD WINNER "The Home By The Sea")

31

*Not only does the placement of furniture define the
separate areas in this room, but the small geometric
print on the chairs and pillows serves a dual purpose. It
helps to define the area for eating and ties it to the other
area of the room, thus creating a feeling of unity, which
of course, contributes to the illusion of spaciousness.
The small scale of the furniture and print also helps.
(Courtesy of Window Shade Manufacturers Association
and Brenemann Shades)*

The walls of a tiny area seem to visually extend well beyond its limited space by the use of mirrors. Here smoky mirrors are used in an angled hallway and a feeling of depth is created with the reflection of the soft flower-covered wallpaper and the statue.
(BURLINGTON HOUSE 1970 AWARD—A SMALL MANHATTAN APARTMENT)

SOURCES OF INFORMATION

Baughman, Milo, "A Designer Shapes Space," *House and Garden*, April 1969.

Hall, Edward and Mildred, *The Hidden Dimension*, Doubleday and Company, New York, 1966.

Hall, Edward and Mildred, "The Language of Personal Space," *House and Garden*, April 1969.

Hall, Edward T., "Proxemics—The Anthropology of Space," *Man in a Changing Environment—New Concepts of time, beauty, space, and social relations.* Proceedings of a one-day institute sponsored by the New York State College of Home Economics at Cornell University, April 18, 1967.

Sommers, Robert, *Personal Space*, The Behavioral Basis of Design, Prentice-Hall, Inc. Englewood Cliffs, N.J., 1969.

PLANNING FURNISHINGS TO MEET HUMAN NEEDS

Furnishing a home need not be difficult if one understands that basically the furnishings in a home have a very definite function — to help the family and individuals living there to carry on the many activities necessary and desirable in meeting their needs for day-to-day living.

Each family develops its own life-style, based on its values, goals, and resources. Wants, needs, and activities will vary for the different areas in a home accordingly.

A plan for furnishings developed step by step according to activities that are related to needs can solve the major problem of what furnishings are needed, and how they need to be arranged.

This plan might be developed in four steps:
☐ Analysis of the area and the activities carried on in it.
☐ Analysis of needs for furnishings to carry out each activity.
☐ Decision on how best to arrange furnishings for each activity for safety, efficiency, and ease, and to meet minimum physical and psychological space requirements.
☐ Analysis of the relationship of various activities to one another in the area to determine where best to place the furnishings for each activity.

Consideration of family values within the framework of the plan should be an integral part of the decisions. So, too, should a concern for the developmental needs of the individuals in the family. As each step of the plan emerges, a critical analysis will include alternatives as well as opportunities for individuals in the family to express preferences. In providing family members with decision-making opportunities, remember that there must also be room for mistakes and for facing up to the

35

consequences of poor decisions. Thus any plan, no matter how basic, must be flexible enough to meet current needs and to adapt to changes as they come along.

1. Analysis of Area and the Activities Carried on in It. It is best to think of home in terms of areas, instead of rooms, since it is the activities unique to the individual family that should determine the furnishings, not the preconceived idea of what rooms must be reserved for each activity.

Although the activities may be centered in rooms traditionally assigned to them, they should be considered objectively in relation to basic living functions.

This thinking process is an important first step in overcoming one of the "hang ups" about how a home should be furnished.

Therefore, the first step in planning the furnishings for a home is to think through the major living areas in the home and to make a list of the activities usually associated with these areas.

In doing so, these questions might be considered:

Why are these activities focused in this particular area? Are there other areas in the home that might be more suitable?

What basic needs is each activity trying to satisfy? Whose needs will be satisfied by it? Will the needs of more than one family member be involved? Is it a creative activity?

Is this an individual or group activity?

Is the activity one unique to the individual family, or is it a traditional concept?

Does the cultural heritage of the family influence the relationship of certain activities to each major living area? How important is this as a factor? Is it meaningful, or a habit that has not been questioned objectively?

As an example, the list might be developed like this:

Major Living Area	Basic Activities	What Basic Needs Being Satisfied	Activities Reflecting Individual or Family Values	Alternatives

Food preparation	Cooking
	Mixing and Baking
	Washing:
	  Foods
	  Dishes
	  Utensils
	Storing:
	  Foods
	  Utensils
	  Ingredients
	  Cleaning
	    supplies
		Hunger
		Thirst
		For individual working in area, could also satisfy self-respect, recognition, self-actualization
			Eating area included
			Telephone Correspondence, Bills at desk
			Preparation and cleanup time planned for interaction of some family members
			Play corner for baby
				Some food preparation might be done outdoors or occasionally in some other area of the home.
				Opportunities for interaction may be planned for other activities in the home

Are there alternatives to this activity?
Once the list of activities, basic and personally desirable, is made, the next step is:

2. An Analysis of the Needs for Furnishings to Carry Out Each Activity. Here is where one needs to think through, step by step, what is involved in carrying out each activity, and to list in detail, all the furnishings needed.

In doing so, these are things to think about:
What furnishings are predetermined by traditional concepts and which are truly basic?
Are all family values in relation to these activities indicative of what is important to them or are some of them part of a traditional concept that has been accepted without question? Are some really for impression of others?
Are the family members involved in the activity helping to think through the needs?
Where are the opportunities for individual growth and development?
Which needs are basic and which are flexible?
Is there a need to compromise any family values in developing this list of needs? Will present resources be adequate to meet the needs for each activity? If not, can a list of priorities be developed?
Can some of these furnishings needs serve a dual purpose with another activity?
Are all furnishings listed as needed really functionally necessary?
Is there a way to encourage creativity in the furnishings planned for each activity?

This list might be twofold with one part prepared very objectively, listing all basic needs, generically and the other part prepared more subjectively, reflecting individual and family values and wants.

Activity	Basic Generic Needs of Furnishings	Individual Values and Wants	Alternatives
Eating	Table, chairs or other suitable facilities on which to serve and eat Dishes, glasses, or some other suitable receptacles for different types of food Source of light Utensils with which to eat	All family members to eat evening meals together Napkins Place mats Candles, Centerpiece Place for food to be cooked and served at the table Art objects in area Floor covering Storage for accessories Special accessories to be used for occasions of recognition for individual family members and holidays	Family forum planned for pre-determined day of week instead of family eating together each day Some informal meals planned on trays Snack bar for quick meals by busy individuals Accessories could be accumulated over a period of years as souvenirs of family trips

The lists will be individual ones for each family. It is important that the step-by-step analysis make one understand and determine what furnishings will be needed for each activity, which are wanted, and what the alternatives are.

3. Decision on How Best to Arrange Furnishings for Each Activity for Safety, Efficiency, Ease, and Minimum Physical and Psychological Space Requirements. The arrangement of furnishings is most important. It affects the organization and direction of each activity, and can contribute to efficiency. Furthermore, it can serve as the screen to protect individuals from overstimulation of the senses by the outside world, as well as by different family members in the home.

Once a generic list of furnishings is made for each activity (or for the activities for each area), then a plan must be developed to determine where the furnishings for each activity are best placed, how much space will be needed to carry it out, what the traffic flow in and around the activity will be. At this point, an honest appraisal of whether or not the area planned for the activity is the most suitable might be in order. An appraisal might also include a consideration of the following:

In a step-by-step analysis of the activity, what motions are involved, which furnishings are utilized by each motion, how much room does each need?

What would happen if another individual walked by while this activity was being carried out? Would there be room? Would it disturb the activity?

Are there any sharp edges or cutting surfaces that can create a safety hazard?

How much space is desirable, how much is absolutely essential? Will more than one person be involved in the activity?

Should the activity be carried out facing the rest of the room, or facing a wall, or doesn't it matter?

How can all furnishings for the activity be arranged for efficiency in use of time and motion and to use least amount of energy?

Will others in the area need to be protected from noises or smells that might be uncomfortable for their space bubble? If so, in what way can this be accomplished?

Can the arrangement be aesthetically pleasing as well as functionally sound?

One approach to such a plan might be to develop a series of basic sketches of the desired arrangement of the furnishings to carry out the activity, with notations on space needs and personal preferences. Alternative choices could also be noted. At this point, cultural heritage will enter the decision-making process. Whether a family is a contact or noncontact one for example, may influence how close furnishings are arranged for a given activity, whether they are planned for one person alone, or several to be involved in together.

As an example:
On the facing page, examples of some possible plans for arranging furnishings for a place to eat, along with notes about personal preferences are shown.

Needs To Be Met. *Space for six people to eat together.*

Atmosphere to create feeling of belonging, and participation in family activity; family conversations are usually lively and sometimes even heated.

First Choice Six people to sit at table; 24 inches per person needed for comfort. Prefer rectangular table.

Storage space for two additional chairs will be needed.

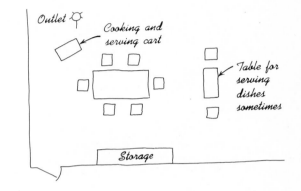

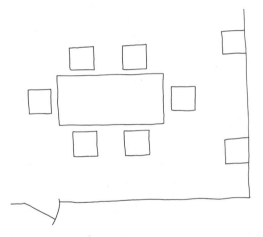

Alternative

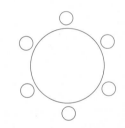

Would like serving cart with space enough to sometimes cook and serve at the table (probably two shelves) so any conversations during mealtime will not be interrupted. Must be placed near electric outlet.

Need space enough for chairs to be pushed back and for individuals to leave the table without causing inconvenience to others seated.

Prefer storage for place mats, flatwear, and some dishes near table—should be near food preparation area where dishes are cleaned.

Would like separate area from which food could be served when formal meals are planned.

Could plan eating area as part of food preparation area and eliminate serving cart; round table might stimulate more lively discussions. For a "contact" family this arrangement might be more desirable.

Could use trays set up in another area of the home; perhaps food could be set up on trays in preparation area and then carried by individuals to eating area; would eliminate serving as part of meal ritual. However, would want to be sure that trays with food on them wouldn't have to be carried too far, or wouldn't create a problem on the way if one should accidentally be dropped.

39

In all these plans, light sources would have to be carefully considered.

If an intimate quiet meal is preferred, candlelight or dim lights would be important. Lively mealtimes, on the other hand, call for a source of bright light (not excluding ample window area).

These, then might be some of the *basic* considerations for the arrangement of furnishings for a family of six for a place to eat. When space requirements are sketched in this way, with alternatives noted, they can help one visualize the needs for each activity, their relationships to one another, and can be the basis for developing a plan for the arrangement of furniture.

At this point, the plan is still an intellectual one, in which the decision-making process is used to evaluate all possible needs and alternatives. The actual arrangement, of course, will need to include consideration of physical space requirements for actual furniture and activities as well as the size and shape of the room to be used.

According to research reported in "Space Standards for Household Activities" published by the Illinois Agricultural Experiment Station, the following space requirements are needed for basic activities in the home. An understanding of these physical space needs can influence decisions about where and how to place furnishings to permit the free flow of traffic from one activity to the other, as well as to provide for the comfort of those involved with the use of the furnishings in day-to-day living.

Space Needed (in Inches)	Activities
16	Edging past seated person
	Cleaning ends of furniture
20	Sitting at table, armless chair
	Foot extension under table
22	Sitting at table, armchair
	Foot extension under desk
	Bedmaking
24	Walking past seated person
26	Walking between wall and table
	Walking between two walls
28	Edging past standing person (12 inches body thickness plus 16 inches edging space)
30	Sitting relaxed in an armless chair
	Rising from chair at folding or typewriter table
32	Rising from table, armless chair
34	Rising from table, armchair
	Forward bend
36	Using desk
	Using bookcase
	Edging past person in armless chair (20 inches sitting space plus 16 inches edging space)
38	Rising from an armless chair in a confined area
	Walking past standing person (12 inches body thickness plus 26 inches walking space)
	Kneeling on one knee
40	Walking with elbows extended
	Using furniture with drawers
	Rising from an armchair in a confined area
42	Using coat closet, one person using file cabinet
52	Two people passing

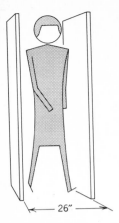

Walking between two high walls (space adequate for both men and women)

Two people passing (figure derived; twice the space for one person to walk between two high walls)

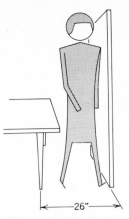

Walking between high wall and 30" high table (space adequate for both men and women)

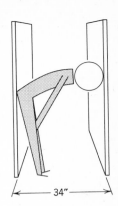

Man bending at a right angle

Kneeling on one knee (woman only)

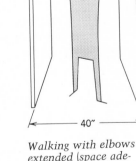

Walking with elbows extended (space adequate for both men and women)

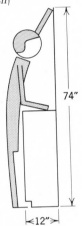
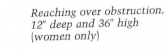

Reaching over obstruction, 12" deep and 36" high (women only)

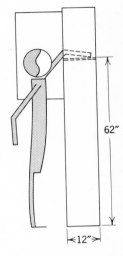

Maximum reach to back of shelf 12" deep (women only)

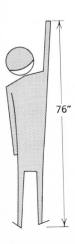

Reaching, maximum height

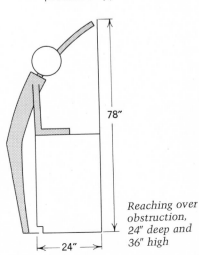

Reaching over obstruction, 24" deep and 36" high

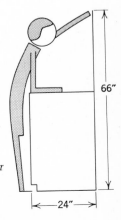

Psychological Needs. We know that personal space needs are as important as actual physical space needs. Although they aren't as easy to measure or define, they must nevertheless be an important consideration in planning the arrangement of furnishings for each activity.

Some things to consider:
Is the family a contact or noncontact family? Are there cultured customs that will influence space use in a given area?

Ervin Goffman indicates that psychologically, people need a stage for performance in a social sense — that they set aside various regions in the environment for frontstage and backstage activities. Frontstage is where the "show" takes place, where socially expected activities are carried out as prescribed; backstage is where the actors (or family members) relax, act as they wish, store some of the props they use to impress guests (such as china, silver, slipcovers with which to cover furniture when it is not being used as part of the show).

In some cultures, the importance of performers can be observed by whether or not their tools are part of the backstage or frontstage. For example, in a German or English home, the cluster of things a woman uses to create the atmosphere and make the "show" are up front; those of an Indian woman are confined to backstage. In American homes, even some so-called backstage areas such as kitchens and bathrooms have become frontstage as a result of increased entertainment in the home.

Are there physical space limitations in the home that may alter ideal psychological space requirements? If so, what compromises are possible, and which must not be compromised?
Do activities of family members require a home to screen overstimulation of senses from the outside world, or is lively space use a need?
Are there different space needs for different age groups and activities in the family? How can these be met in the space available?
Is each activity a group one or an individual one? Can it affect stimulation of the senses of others in the home who are not involved in the activity?

4. Analysis of the Relationship of Various Activities to One Another in the Area to Determine Where Best to Place Furnishings for Each Activity. At this point, it is important to consider not only the generic list of furnishings related to each activity but also the kinds of human relationships that will be encouraged by the environment.

How many different activities must be carried on in the area? How many will be carried on at the same time?
Will the activities call for privacy, or will there be a need or want for people to relate to one another, to communicate? And if so, would all individuals in the family relate to one another in this activity, or just some? Which ones?
Should the furnishings be placed to organize the activities of one group (children, for instance) away from other groups? Or within sight but not sound? Should they be planned for interaction?

42

Can the placement be flexible so that some-
    times it can provide privacy and at other
    times include other people?
Are some activities related so that proximity
    to each other is desirable? If so, how much
    space will be needed for each? Can there be
    any overlapping?
Will the arrangement encourage individuals to
    relate to the activity, or is it a setting into
    which people must fit to carry on what
    they want to do?
An analysis of a place for the family to relax
together might be developed thus:
*TV set needed—must be placed where it can
be seen readily by all in room.*

*Prefer two seating units that can double as
beds when guests come. Want them arranged
to take the least space. Also need two comfortable chairs. Should be arranged so that
everyone can communicate in a group if desired.*

*Need table and several chairs for flexible
uses—study, hobbies, writing letters;—depending on who uses it. Should be placed to
relate to other activities in room, still be
private. Suggest table against wall with
chairs facing wall.*

After the first four steps have been carefully
thought through, the final one will be to select furnishings. Some knowledge of what
functionally is appropriate is important. This
can be a real challenge. So often, we blindly
follow tradition in the selection of furnishings, buying a sofa and two chairs for the
living room, for instance, or matching nite
tables for either side of a bed, when really, we
should be asking ourselves questions such as
those on the next page.

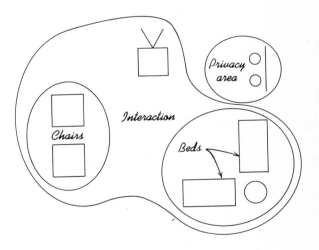

If I didn't have a preconceived idea about what furnishings should be used for each activity, how would I plan what is needed? Could I consider items objectively and evaluate whether or not they could serve the purpose even though they may not have been originally designed for that function?

What function, specifically, does each piece of furniture or accessory need to fulfill in the home?

Is the design suitable to the function?

What are the basic features needed to make it perform efficiently?

Are there extra features on some models? What do they add to the function or beauty? Will the extra features add enjoyment even if they are not necessary to the function?

What about maintenance and care? Are they commensurate with performance and end use expected? Are extra resources needed for upkeep or care?

Does the object meet individual standards for beauty?

Does it reflect the family life-style?

Is durability important in this particular item? If so, how much durability is expected?

These are the personal and practical aspects of the selection of furnishings. But this is only the beginning, for here is where creativity and self-expression, reflecting individual values, taste, and experience comes into play. Beauty is an integral part of function. It contributes the "nourishment for the soul" that can turn an ordinary task into a pleasant one. Beautiful surroundings can also minimize psychological fatigue, providing the setting for relaxation and contemplation of the whole high world with wonder.

Creating beauty in the home is not easy. There is no measure against which to evaluate one's efforts objectively (and thank goodness for that, because our concept of beauty should be a personal one that can grow and change to reflect personal values).

But there are guidelines that have been used over the years to define design which can be studied, not as rules to be followed religiously, but as bench marks against which to evaluate choices in building confidence in one's decisions. (More of this in Design chapters.)

Certainly one of the ways to nurture this confidence is to encourage creativity in the home.

In a home dedicated to helping individuals grow and develop, this can take many forms:

A child planning the decoration for a family member's birthday cake.

A teenager selecting furnishings for some part of the home. (They may not reflect values of the rest of the family, but this selection can be an exercise, in decision making, in self-expression, and can provide an opportunity to learn to understand self, to decide what is important.)

Making something for the home, or perhaps planting a garden.

Careful attention to details everywhere in the home to influence sensitivity to the whole being the sum of its parts. This could include the color of soap for the kitchen or bathroom, the napkins to go with dishes, and the container selected to hold food.

Above all, the real reason for furnishing a home must not be obscured by concern for the selection of appropriate furnishings. Although design and function are important, and beauty adds the spiritual essence to it all, still the real objective for furnishing a home is not to create a setting in which people must fit but, instead, to create an environment with which individuals can identify and which, in turn, can influence the very fiber of humanity in man—love, sensitivity, morality, ethics, emotional expression, and the meeting of his basic needs so that he can reach toward self-actualization.

The next few chapters discuss guidelines for developing plans for furnishing various areas in the home. However, they are only guidelines and sources of ideas, since each home should be unique to the people living there and the furnishings should be planned and selected, ultimately, to meet their needs, to reflect their values and goals.

SOURCES OF INFORMATION

Goffman, E., *The Presentation of Self in Everyday Life*, Doubleday and Company, Garden City, New York, 1959.

Krampen, Martin, "Social Sciences and The Design of Human Environments," a presentation at a one-day institute on *Man in a Changing Environment—New Concepts of Time, Beauty, Space, and Social relations.* Proceedings of a one-day institute sponsored by the New York State College of Home Economics, at Cornell University, April 18, 1967.

McCullough, K. P., Smith, R. H., Wood, A. L., Woolrich, A., "Space Standards for Household Activities," Bulletin 686, University of Illinois Agricultural Experiment Station.

Planning for Privacy

"The right to be let alone — the most comprehensive of rights and the right most valued by civilized men."

Louis Brandeis

The need for privacy is a key to pyschological survival. Individual sanity and self-maintenance depends on it. Although individuals have a need to communicate with others, they also have a need to withdraw, even from communication with members of their family to reaffirm a sense of self-hood. It has been found that "there is a threshold beyond which interaction is unendurable. It is because people frequently take leave of one another that the interaction-linking proposition maintains itself." How individuals are able to regulate and control the way they relate to others has a decided effect on sanity.

The degree to which home provides for privacy is as critical to husbands and wives as it is to individuals. As partners, they need to spend some time alone together each day to communicate. As the psychiatrist, Paul Lemkau, states:

> "Perhaps the first function of a home is to provide a place in which a couple destined for procreation can have a refuge, a place to return to from the world around them. Humans, like birds, want nests of their own."

Husbands and wives need auditory as well as visual privacy to withdraw together, beyond the sight and sound of others.*

* Dr. Paul V. Lemkau, "A Psychiatrist's View of Housing" *Proceedings: Seventh Conference for the Improvement of the Teaching of Housing in Home Economics Land-Grant Colleges and State Universities*, October 30–November 2, 1963. University Park, Pennsylvania, College of Home Economics Publication No. 180, Pennsylvania State University, 1964.

47

Overcrowded homes that do not permit even a moment's privacy for individuals or husbands and wives, force family members to devise their own ways of satisfying this need, and may mean that they have to go outside the home for it. This, of course, can lead to many other problems.

Interestingly, it has been found that children coming from families where this "nesting drive" of husband and wife have been frustrated (from living in crowded quarters) have had psychiatric problems. In some cultures, where it has been customary for generations to live together without much privacy, there is a growing trend among the younger generation to want some privacy.

Many cultures have nourished the need for privacy through customs and behavioral patterns.

Perhaps the most classic example of this is the Japanese garden, no matter how small, with its symbolic beauty that is planned for private contemplation.

The Arabs dress their women in purdah, to shield them from the eyes of others, but indirectly purdah also provides privacy for the individual clothed in it.

In Japan, people may be invisible even though they can be seen. According to their code of ethics, if a hostess is not ready to see a guest, she is invisible. She may come into the room but not be "seen" until she is ready to greet her guest.

Privacy implies relief from overstimulation as well as from interaction. Certainly noise in the form of unwanted sound is one form of this. If prolonged, unwanted noise can effect one's peace of mind and mental tranquility. In fact, the United States Public Health

Service points out that noise can build stress and nervousness, impair hearing, affect sleep, reduce work productivity, and interfere with the understanding of speech, or even with convalescence.

There is a fine distinction between noise and sound, and it is a very personal one. What's noise to one person may be a beautiful sound to another—music, for example, or the sound of children at play. It all depends on one's frame of reference. And although an individual may not always be aware of the noise around him, it can create fatigue, irritability, anxiety, and tension.

According to Dr. Chauncey Leake, University of California, San Francisco, excess noise not only affects the nervous, endocrine, and reproductive systems, but it may damage unborn children. Even sounds that we enjoy, such as the crowds at an athletic event, music at a concert, or the force of a waterfall can be harmful, if they are too loud, or if individuals are exposed to them too long.

A decibel scale (db) is used to measure sound pressure level. Every 10 degree increase brings a corresponding increase in pressure of 10 times. Some (db) levels of sounds familiar to most people are:

Shotgun Blast	140 db
Amplified Rock Band, Jet Airport	120 db
Noisy Kitchen, Subway Train	100 db
Power Lawn Mower	95 db
Food Blender, Noisy Exhaust Fan	90 db
Vacuum Cleaner	87 db
Garbage Disposal Unit, Knife Sharpener	80 db
Dishwasher	70 db
Normal Conversation	60 db
Refrigerator	45 db

The large windows in this city apartment have been designed for sound and light control with double window shades placed to go from the bottom up and from the top down. Fabric draperies, a wall hanging, and wall to wall carpeting also help to control noise. Noise pollution, especially in cities, can be a real problem in the pursuit of privacy.
(Courtesy Window Shade Manufacturers Association)

Whisper	30 db
Breathing	10 db
Lowest Audible Sound	0 db

According to most authorities, the (db) range can be described as follows:

100 to 140 db — Deafening
80 to 100 db — Very Loud
60 to 80 db — Loud
40 to 60 db — Moderate
20 to 40 db — Faint
0 to 20 db — Very Faint

Prolonged exposure to sound level above the 60 db level can be harmful. It's interesting to note that a number of household appliances, in the normal course of operation, are above this level.

A study recently carried out at the University of Wisconsin Department of Environmental Design, indicates that unexpected noise levels in the home can cause accidents. Because these noises cause stress, they can also contribute to irritability and depression on the part of individuals and even a breakdown in family communications.

Noise can be controlled to a degree in these ways:

By the use of sound absorbing materials such as acoustical tile, wall-to-wall carpeting, full curtains or draperies that go from ceiling to floor, wall hangings, and upholstered furniture.

By lining walls near the source of noise with clothes closets or bookcases filled with books, since books and clothes are good absorbers of sound.

By the use of double windows if necessary.

By using carpeting or rubber mats on stairs.

By lining shelves with a material, such as cork, which will minimize sounds when items are removed.

By filling all holes in walls (e.g. areas around pipes) to minimize sounds traveling from one room to another

By making certain that all appliances are level so they do not vibrate or touch another unit when in motion.

By lowering the ceiling, if the height of the room permits, to have a suspended ceiling of sound absorbing material.

By changing the sound levels of telephones, doorbells, and buzzers if they are annoying. Silent electric wall switches are also available.

By using insulation devices wherever possible around appliances which might be noisy, such as window air conditioning units, garbage disposals.

According to the National Institute for Occupational Health and Safety a person should not be exposed to sound levels above 90 db for more than one hour in twenty four. Noting the db of familiar sounds on the previous page, this seems almost an impossibility.

Planning for privacy, then, becomes another one of the primary concerns in furnishing a home. One of the common misconceptions about privacy is that only a room of one's own can provide for this need. Not so. There are many ways that a home can be planned for the privacy of individuals. And privacy can take more than one form. For example, a degree of privacy can be achieved by withdrawing from the auditory factors in the environment. How?

A hair dryer, used in any area of the home, can for a brief period provide a "legitimate"

51

A family room with flexible furnishings may provide opportunities for individuals to rearrange furnishings to achieve a degree of privacy watching TV, desk work, gazing out the window, sitting absorbed in one's own thoughts.
1971 BURLINGTON HOUSE AWARD WINNER —
(Photo Courtesy of House & Garden
Remodeling Guides © *1970 Conde Nast Publications, Inc.)*

reason for not communicating or interacting with others, for being alone with one's thoughts, for shutting out the other sounds in the environment.

A stereo or other source of music can be used to drown out all other auditory stimuli, to leave one engulfed in a world of music. Of course, this same factor may also become "noise" to other members of the family. Perhaps, a respect for the privacy needs of individual family members might make this "noise" tolerable for a while by others who are not finding it their source of escape into privacy. If the home is crowded, a mutual understanding might be arranged about the length of time that this "noise" can be used, at any one time, for escape by the individual. And if it is just plain intolerable, or if the home is in an apartment building with thin walls, perhaps, an earphone plugged into a unit is the solution to music for privacy without noise pollution for others.

The role of television in the home as a tool for privacy cannot be overlooked either. Sports events can be a time when family members understand that a member of the family is not to be disturbed. Or, for that matter, favorite programs of any family members can be their time to "tune out" other family members or responsibilities, even though there may be other activities going on in the room.

All three of these means of auditory privacy provide a legitimate escape for the individual involved, without fostering feelings of guilt.

The same can be achieved for visual privacy, too.

An ordinary task like peeling potatoes or washing dishes, can turn into a haven for privacy, especially if the kitchen is small and

When there's not enough space for each individual to have a personal refuge for privacy, some work areas in the home may serve as substitutes. For example, a tiny kitchen, with room only for one person at a time to work, can be an ideal place to be alone, while a chore such as dish washing or food preparation can serve as a reason to get away from others without feeling guilty. (Courtesy Window Shade Manufacturers Association)

there is room for only one person at a time.

Or, responsibility for weeding the garden can be a valid reason to be alone.

A chair or desk area placed somewhat apart from the others in a room, can be an oasis to sit and read, or just relax, away from everyone in the family. Some chairs are especially well designed to contribute to this need — they seem to reach out and enfold those who choose to sit in them. The wing chair is a classic example.

Furniture can be arranged to allow for areas of privacy also.

A more ideal form of privacy is, of course, a room or area of one's own where it is possible to really be alone to refresh one's soul. But this area can only be effective if it encourages self-expression and involvement by the individual for whom it is intended. The novel, *The Kitchen Madonna*, by Rumer Godden is the story of a family cook and the little shrine that she made for herself in the kitchen, with a jeweled figure she brought from her home country. This was her very personal area in the kitchen, the sancum sanctorum she turned to for collecting her thoughts and nourishing her soul!

Ideally, privacy means not only a way to be alone when it is necessary, but the freedom to make mistakes or carry out tasks without the entire family or neighborhood looking over one's shoulder. This means planning adequate space for the activities carried out by all family members. In a home where there are school-age children, an important consideration is facilities for study where there will not be undue interruptions from too many family members carrying out individual pursuits in the same area.

Certain basic necessities are generic:

A flat surface on which to write or work.
Supplies for work.
A place to put discards (wastebasket).
A light source.

To contribute to efficiency in work, all should be within easy reach. Most people will want a study area that can be relatively free from distractions.

Although some would consider it prudish, many individuals do feel that bathroom privacy is important in the home. In a large family with limited living space this is not always easy to accomplish.

If the washing facilities are sufficiently separate from the toilet, a separator of some kind can be used to provide a measure of privacy. This could be a bookcase that serves a dual role as a storage unit and a room divider; or a long curtain, such as a plastic shower curtain, might be hung from the ceiling to form a partition.

Another approach might be to analyze just what activities are carried on in the bathroom:

Which ones could be done in another area of the house (make-up, for instance)?

Which ones could be done in "off hours" when there is less demand for the bathroom by family members (washing clothes, for instance)?

Could the organization of supplies speed up the time needed in bathing or washing (for example, planning the storage of towels and grooming aids at point of use)?

On the following pages, some approaches to creating privacy in the home are discussed and illustrated. Ultimately, how the human need for privacy is met is a problem to be solved according to individual situations.

*The need for individual family members to get away
from it all for brief periods of time is one of the most
important needs home can fulfill. Sometimes this can be
accomplished simply by planning for a quiet corner in
an area such as a porch or patio where anyone can sit
and commune with self or nature for a brief period of
time.*
(Courtesy Window Shade Manufacturers Association)

56

In some city homes that are really one large room, privacy can be hard to come by. This may create a real strain, even though a couple is married and enjoys togetherness. An area divider (pictured on the left) created by a free standing screen can simulate some degree of privacy by separating the sleeping area from the rest of the room.

(Courtesy HOUSE BEAUTIFUL)

Pictured below, a bedroom shared by two is planned to provide a degree of privacy by the arrangement of the beds, head to head, separated by a louvre panel that goes from floor to ceiling.

(Courtesy J.C. Penney Company, Inc.)

For a busy career person sharing a first apartment, or maybe renting a room in a home, privacy could mean a bedsitting room to go to when one wants to be alone to read or think. It could be the only refuge from the many outside worlds of work, new friends, new environment. (*1971 BURLINGTON HOUSE AWARD WINNER submitted by Eidth Coogler* Atlanta Journal)

A room to pursue one's hobbies, away from the curiosity and intrusions of others and where one can be as messy as one wants without fear of offending others is a real luxury. This painting studio (pictured on the right) with its own sky light is just such a haven of privacy. (*1971 BURLINGTON HOUSE AWARD "The Nantucket Home" submitted by Martha J. Walters* The Nantucket Inquirer—Mirror)

This contemporary study bedroom is in a corner room of an old apartment has been planned for privacy from sight and sound, as well as a refuge for the pursuit of personal interests. The window shades, function to screen out noise as well as light. Books in a unit from floor to ceiling also help to absorb sounds. (Courtesy Window Shade Manufacturers Association)

60

In a home with too much family in a limited space, the bathroom may present the biggest challenge in planning for privacy. One approach, especially for a home with young children, is to separate the washing area from the bathing area. Towels and grooming needs can be organized on shelves, with a separate one assigned to each individual for further recognition of each person having an area he can call his own, even in the bathroom. The illustration on this page and the one following is an artist's rendering of how this might be achieved with imagination.
(Courtesy J.C. Penney Company, Inc.)

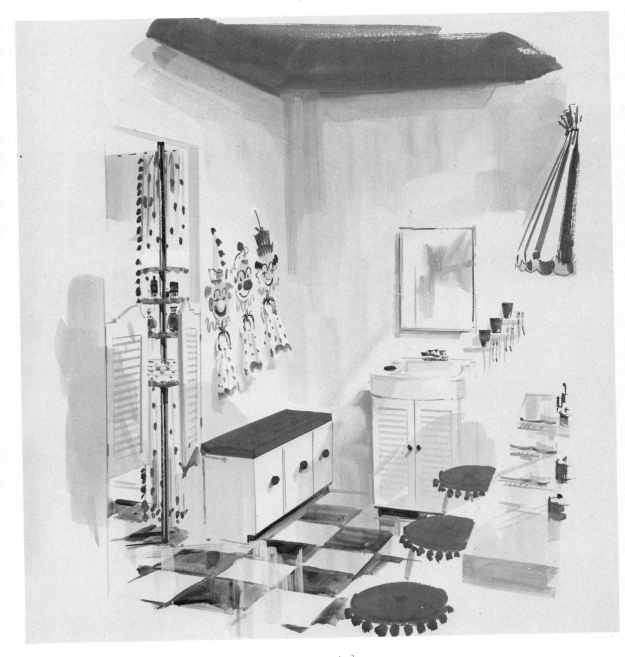

62

SOURCES OF INFORMATION

Cobb, Betsy and Hubbard, "Noise Control
    Begins at Home," WOMAN'S DAY,
    March 1972, p. 42.
Lemkau, Paul V., M.D., "A Psychiatrist's View
    of Housing" *Proceedings: Seventh Confer-
    ence for the Improvement of the Teaching
    of Housing in Home Economics Land-
    Grant Colleges and State Universities*,
    October 30–November 2, 1963. University
    Park, Pennsylvania, College of Home Eco-
    nomics Publication No. 180, Pennsylvania
    State University, 1964.
Montgomery, James E., "Impact of Housing
    Patterns on Marital Interaction," *The Fam-
    ily Coordinator*, July 1970, pp. 267–274.
Watts, Joanne, *The Woman's Guide to the
    Orient*, published by Japan Air Lines ©
    1970.

Areas for Socialization, Interaction, Relaxation

The need for interaction between human beings is a powerful one. In fact, Erich Fromm states that failure to achieve interpersonal fusion can mean insanity or destruction of self or others.

The family, of course, is a primary source for learning socialization, and home as the environment for the family has the potential to provide for unlimited opportunities for interaction. This takes thoughtful planning, especially since several factors in society today seem to be limiting this interaction potential:

Segregation by age
Mobility that separates the nuclear family
    from the extended family
Technological advances that have brought
    about stereotyped impersonal services and
    standardization of human behavior and
    responses in some situations.

Current research seems to indicate that if society continues to separate adults from active participation in the lives of children, and if the resulting vacuum is filled by peer groups divorced from the rest of society, that we can anticipate increased alienation, indifference, antagonism, and violence on the part of the younger generation in all segments of society, including middle class as well as disadvantaged. The solution seems to be in trying to bring about the greater involvement of adults and children in each others lives and responsibilities.*

Although family structure has been undergoing change with experiments such as

* Urie Brofenbrenner, "Who Makes The Generation Gap?" Penney's *Forum*, Spring and Summer 1968.

communal living, no social institution has yet been found to substitute for it. Therefore, the first place to start in planning for interaction continues to be the family and its home.

The family has been described as a corporate unit of interacting and interdependent personalities who have a common theme and goals, have commitment over time, and share resources and a common living space. It is an environment for the individual as well as a unit existing in a larger physical and social environment.* This environment for the individual, which the family provides, is not just physical, but psychological and social as well; it is one in which reciprocal effects of individuals within the family take place at and among all age levels.

Ideally, a strong family, is made up of these components: †

The ability to provide for the physical, emotional, and spiritual needs of its members.
The ability to be sensitive to the needs of its members.
The ability to communicate.
The ability to provide support, security, and encouragement.
The ability to establish and maintain growth-producing relationships within and without the family.
The ability to grow with and through children.
The capacity to maintain and create constructive and responsible community relationships in the neighborhood and in the

school, town, and state governments.
An ability for self-help, and the ability to accept help when appropriate.
An ability to perform family roles flexibly.
Mutual respect for the individuality of family members.
A concern for family unity, loyalty, and inter-family cooperation.

Home as the environment that houses the family can be planned deliberately to encourage opportunities for the interaction and interdependence involved in the development of these components.

First, it must be recognized that interaction does not involve family members alone. Friends and guests also play a part. And families do use home and its furnishings to make a statement about their values and their life-style. To a degree, this impression value is important in setting the stage for interaction. But it must still be an honest impression if it is to help the individuals in the family relate to it, even as a background for socialization. Homes that become show places for company, with museumlike rooms furnished for display, not only inhibit interaction, they also indirectly say to the family that outsiders are more important than family members.

Interaction involves more than people. It may sometimes take place when a person interacts with an object, a piece of art, an idea, a gift from someone who is loved, an object associated with a happy memory, or an antique that has roots with the past.

Or, it may be a combination of both elements—the object and the people, such as a game, a musical instrument, ornaments for the Christmas tree or, a television set that involves them in sports or drama.

---

* Nancy C. Hook and Beatrice Paolucci, "The Family as an Ecosystem," *Journal of Home Economics* Vol. 62, No. 5, May 1970, pp. 315–318.
† Herbert Otto, "What Is A Strong Family?" *Marriage and Family Living*, Vol. XXIV, No. 1, February 1962.

66

This old carving of an oriental figure has a prominent place in the home of Dr. Verda Dale. It is a source of inspiration, a work of art which she can enjoy. Literally interpreted, interaction between an inanimate object and a human probably cannot take place, because there is no mutual influence. However, the feelings of a person toward an object, especially one of significance emotionally, can often be more than mere reaction. It's response to something that touches the soul and how can this really be defined? (Courtesy Dr. Verda Dale)

Some of the Potential for Interaction
Areas that Encourage Communication:

Comfortable seating, arranged so that individuals can make eye contact combined with easy access to food to nibble can be an excellent setting to encourage conversation.
"Environment 70," a grouping designed by Milo Baughman provides just such a background. The unit can be arranged to leave an entrance of two feet. A table in the center has a fixed lacquered central core with a rosewood rotating rim.
(Courtesy Thayer Coggin, Inc.)

*Communication need not always be verbal. Sometimes
there can be meaningful interaction when people are in
the same room, involved in a personal pursuit. They can
be communicating in silence, each taking comfort in
knowing that the other is there, feeling the warm
satisfaction of "belonging" and of being loved. A noncontact family might be quite happy in a room like this
where areas for activities are clearly defined and
separate, yet near enough for silent communication.
(Courtesy Window Shade Manufacturers Association)*

A bedroom planned with space for writing, sitting, or watching TV can encourage nonverbal communication. (Burlington House 1970 Award — THE EFFICIENCY APARTMENT)

Games are fun and they can be such a natural tool for interation among many different age groups. They can serve as a situation for an older family member to teach a young one a new skill; they can be the setting for friendly competition among siblings; they can be the background for people to share ideas and opinions. Planning the props into the furnishings in the area can only serve to encourage interaction.
(Courtesy of Wallcovering Industry Bureau)

Areas That Encourage Interpersonal Relations among Age Groups:

The editors of LADIES' HOME JOURNAL designed this family activity center (opposite page) which includes the food preparation area as well as a place for eating, entertainment, and hobbies. The maximum flexibility in how the furnishings can be used creates a setting to encourage human beings to relate to one another, even while they carry on individual pursuits.

Two areas concealed by folding doors open up into one center for housing sewing equipment and supplies, and another for TV, stereo and records, film and camera gear. Most of the furniture is on casters so it can be easily moved to form whatever groupings are best for the moment.

(Reprinted by special permission of LADIES' HOME JOURNAL copyright 1970 Downe Publishing Company, Inc.)

Photography by Jerry Abramowitz.

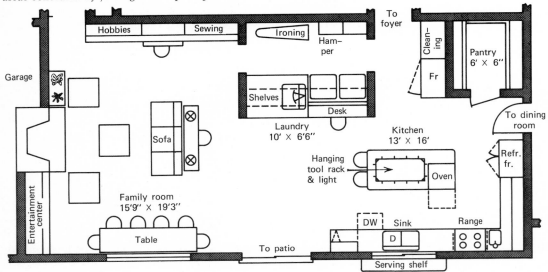

73

A place for lively socialization and relaxation is important, too, where family or friends can enjoy each other without feeling inhibited by furnishings that seem perishable. Sometimes this takes place best in a family room, other times in the traditional living room furnished for "front stage."

This room was designed with active family members in mind. The furniture is resistant to sticky fingers and coverings can be wiped easily.

(Courtesy J.C. Penney Company, Inc.)

Carefully planned, a food preparation area can encourage many different kinds of interaction. If some family members have responsibilities for food preparation, or clean up after a meal, it can be the setting for a way to learn to relate to another human being. If there is room for play, children can learn to relate to adults while they each are involved in carrying out their respective activities.
(*Reprinted by special permission of LADIES' HOME JOURNAL, Downe Publishing, Inc.*)

(*Opposite page*)
One family has placed the piano adjacent to the food preparation area to encourage interaction. Why not? Thinking through human needs may well challenge traditional concepts of where furnishings should be placed in the home.
(*Courtesy HOUSE BEAUTIFUL*)

Furnishings can be planned to foster:

The use of the family home by individual members for school, church, or political activities to encourage involvement and responsibility in community affairs. This implies pride in home, too, so that involvement by family members in decisions relating to the furnishing of areas that are "front stage" is important if they are to want to bring others home.

This type of planning could accomplish more than one purpose. If the family includes grandparents it can provide an opportunity to show youth that older folks are worth living with for their strength, experience, and wisdom. If carefully planned, it can also bring about a feeling of self-respect and worthiness needed by the aged ones. Both groups can learn from each other and can influence each other, too.

It may also be a way to help young people to appreciate and understand male and female roles. Daughters usually have many opportunities to identify with the female role in observing mother in the home. Sons, however, may not have as much opportunity, since the father usually is away at work during the day. Carefully planned opportunities for young men and women to observe mother and father "at work" in their roles in the home can especially clarify the male role of:

Emotional support and companionship for the wife.
A model for daughters to observe and learn attitudes, feelings, and expectations toward men.
A model of a male adult for boys in the family.
This implies a father who acts as a male

adult with the boys, not one who tries to be a peer.

Shared Responsibilities. Mutual respect is a factor in interpersonal relations. Shared responsibilities can be the setting for its development. However, responsibilities must be meaningful with an opportunity for decision making, and they should be related to areas of the home that are shared by the family where recognition from family members will be apparent.

It has been suggested that one reason high school girls do not like housework is that they have too little rather than too much real responsibility. Parents all too often delegate to children those tasks that get little recognition, with regard to value, for adults—things like clearing the table and doing the dishes for girls or, for boys, emptying the garbage.*

A Place To Dream, To Enjoy Beauty. How many homes provide family members with an environment in which they can take time to enjoy beauty, to wonder at a star, to waste time, if they choose, or to give meaning to their responsibilities? Planning a setting for this kind of interaction between people and their environment requires an understanding of individual concepts of beauty and what will create a response for each. One place may not fill the needs for all. A variety of opportunities for interaction between people and objects may be the answer.

The opportunities for meaningful inter-

---

* Evelyn Millis Duvall, "High School Girls and the Tasks of Homemaking," Research Finds, *Marriage and Family Living,* November 1960.

personal relationships within the home can be many if home is furnished to be a living breathing environment in which there is room for families to be boisterous or active, if they choose, to quarrel if necessary, to engage in some spontaneous activity, or to indulge in the uninhibited expression of feelings.

To a degree, homes have been furnished for socialization and relaxation, but they have been confined within the concepts of the traditional living room, family room or, perhaps, the den. These limited traditional concepts cannot embrace new approaches to building an environment for human interaction. They are based on the behavior patterns of another era when the family lived within the framework of a different way of life. They reflect the accumulated influences of environment and history, woven together into an intricate design of living patterns known as culture.

How much does this influence today's home? A look at how other cultures plan their areas for socialization and interaction and a study of the part that tradition plays in all of this, can help families gain insight into how their values for these areas are developed.

Perhaps the classic example, still influencing how homes are furnished for socialization today, is the Victorian era.

The Victorian home was furnished to reflect the new preoccupation with mass production—when furnishings formerly made by skilled craftsmen could be quickly copied and turned out by machine. It was an age of copying—not dishonestly, but for the joy of recognizing the achievement of the human mind that had invented machinery to do the same work as was once done by hand, in much less time. They were fascinated by imitations of carvings, semiprecious stones, wood graining, and prepared furniture with curves rather than straight lines. They also delighted in the new use of materials for furniture—for example, brass for beds. In "front stage" areas, especially the parlor, Victorians loved novelty gadgets and ingenious devices by which furniture could serve several purposes. Their rigid "rules" for proper behavior also influenced how home was furnished and used by the family.

The stamp of the Victorian parlor can still be seen on many of today's homes. The name has been changed to living room, but its function remains, for all intents and purposes, that of a formal room for receiving and entertaining guests. And some of the traditional furniture, a sofa, two matching chairs, and small tables, also remains.

Traditional rules plays a major role, too, in influencing family homes, and their areas for interaction and socialization.

In many homes in Japan, today, for example, the main room of the home planned for socialization is furnished according to tradition. Furnishings are sparse, with cushions for seating at the low table. Pictures are hung high on the wall, planned for viewing from a seated position on the floor. A semisacred alcove (tokonoma) is the focal point with its objects of beauty to be enjoyed. This may include a scroll that is changed with the seasons, as well as one or two objects of beauty and a simple floral arrangement. The floor is covered with tatami (3-inch thick straw mats).

Elaborate rules govern behavior in the room. Shoes must be removed when entering a room with tatami floors and shoes must be left pointed in the direction from which the visitor came.

The seat of honor in this main room is in

front of the tokonoma. One doesn't sit there unless invited to do so. In fact, one must sit nearest the door, the humblest position in the room, until invited to sit elsewhere by the host or hostess.

The overall effect is one of calm and beauty, and disciplined behavior.

Some main rooms may have a Shinto shrine, high on the wall, for the worship of ancestors, with a place for offerings. Here, family members can interact with the memory of their ancestors (whose pictures are in the shrine) to ask for special favors.

Sometimes climate is an influence — in countries with warmer climates, courtyards are the center of activity and family interaction, although most homes also have more formal rooms for entertaining or socialization with those outside the family.

Homes in India have open courtyards surrounded by bedrooms. Here, in the warm morning sun, the women of the family prepare vegetables for cooking, children play, and father shaves while having his morning tea.

Furnishings invite long cozy chats, with many wicker chairs and several charpoys (rope beds used for sitting as well as lying).

When guests come to call, they are taken to a more formal sitting room and children are sent to their bedrooms where they are not seen and not heard. If there are a number of guests, the men and women usually separate and sit on opposite sides of the room, each group discussing topics appropriate to their interests.

This formal room usually is a "front stage" area for family status, and such status symbols as electrical appliances, the refrigerator, and innumerable plastic knickknacks are proudly displayed.

Perhaps the real challenge to today's families is to clarify their own values about what is important and to meld the meaningful rituals of tradition and culture with their comtemporary needs.

But this must be done with care. Every family is unique. The type of interaction and its frequency will vary from family to family.

To plan for it, one must consider:
The size of the family.
The age span of the family.
The number of generations living together.
The kind and amount of space available indoors and outdoors.

Is the family more inclined toward active or passive activities?
Which family members are the most active?
In what types of activities?
Are any family members home all day? How many?
What ages? What relationship?
Are all family members home most evenings? Which ones are not? Why?
Are there any outside activities that the family is actively involved in as a group — that is, politics, church, school, or social club?
Is home a screen from the outside world, or the place where the action is?

Are family members contact or noncontact people?
Extroverts or introverts?
How close are family members? Does a feeling of interdependence already exist?
Is the relationship warm and friendly? Reserved? Indifferent?
Which members are "closest"?
Is the influence of the cultural heritage of the family prominent or subtle?

80

A Japanese Tokonoma
(Courtesy Japan National Tourist Association)

A shrine for worshipping ancestors in a Japanese home.
(Courtesy Japan National Tourist Organization)

81

Potential for Interaction

What size are those areas where interaction with other family members or guests might take place? Is there space enough for several people to be together?

To what degree does interaction now exist in the family?

If there is no appreciable interaction among family members, what seems to be the reason?

What activities could be used to begin to bring together some family members of different age groups?

Is there space for more than one activity to be carried on at the same time in the area?

What family members need to interact with each other more? How can responsibilities be realigned to create an opportunity for this to happen? Where in the home will it happen? What furnishings will be needed?

If there isn't enough opportunity for interaction of family members alone, what types of opportunities can be made for visitors also to be involved with the family?

Do the furnishings in the home now encourage interaction? If not, why?

Are there objects with which individuals might interact?

Arrangement of Furnishings for Activities. In an area planned for socialization, the attention to physical space needs is especially important. There must be adequate space for people to function effectively so that the real reason for the environment, *interaction,* is not lost in a maze of furniture groupings that one must stumble over, walk through or around to go from one activity to the other.

Some activities can be pursued productively adjacent to one another, others may require isolation or lots of room to spread out; the amount of space needed for each must be carefully planned in assigning space.

Traffic patterns must be carefully analyzed, too, not only in relation to how one walks through the room, but where each activity is placed in relation to doors that may open in or out, to the amount of natural light needed, and to the relative quiet desirable.

Physical Space Needs. Some basic requirements, established by research are:

Space Needs for Armless Chair 20″×21″

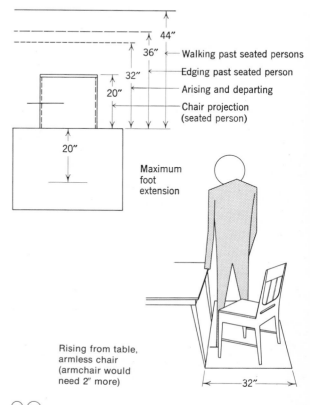

44″
36″ ← Walking past seated persons
32″ ← Edging past seated person
20″ ← Arising and departing
Chair projection (seated person)

20″

Maximum foot extension

Rising from table, armless chair (armchair would need 2″ more)

32″

Space Needs with Armchair 22″×23″

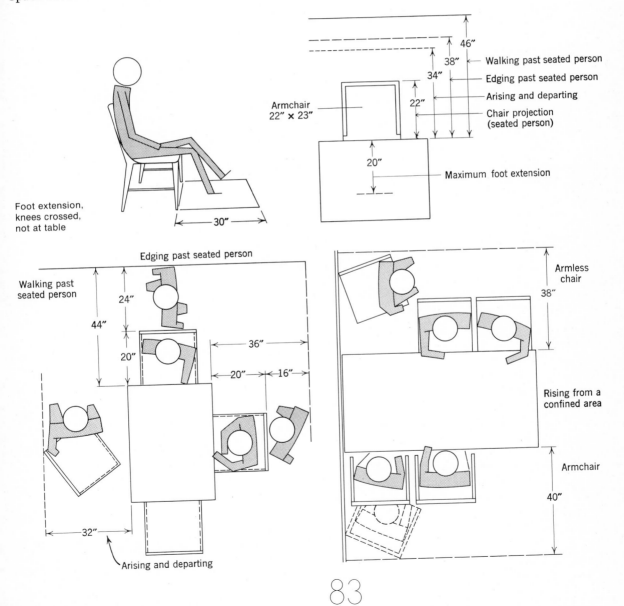

Foot extension,
knees crossed,
not at table

Armchair
22″ × 23″

46″
38″ ← Walking past seated person
34″ ← Edging past seated person
22″ ← Arising and departing
Chair projection
(seated person)

20″ — Maximum foot extension

30″

Edging past seated person

Walking past
seated person

24″

44″

20″

36″

20″ 16″

32″

Arising and departing

Armless
chair

38″

Rising from a
confined area

Armchair

40″

83

Psychological Space Needs. Psychological space needs cannot be ignored either, especially in an area shared by many. The need for the privacy of the individual space bubble is always present.

It's important to think about:
Territoriality.

How many family members will have favorite furnishings or sections in the area to which they will "lay claim"? Does the area have enough room for this to take place? And can furnishings be arranged to accommodate this pattern and still provide environment for interaction?

If pets are an important part of the family, is there space for them to have their own "territories"?

Overstimulation of the senses.

How much sound, smell, and touch will activities in the area create?

Is the area adjacent to another where some of these sensory stimulants might originate? Is there any way to screen out undesirable noise, smell, or touch? Are some of these sensory stimulants desirable to encourage interactions?

Will these stimulants be desirable to some and not-so-desirable to others who might use the same area? (Different types of music, for example, and different levels of sound related to it.) Although interaction implies informal and spontaneous communication, perhaps some planning may be called for in situations where stimulation of the senses to one person may be overstimulation to another.

Individual space needs.

Is the area flexible enough for noncontact and contact people?

Is there enough space to accommodate space bubbles of guests as well as the family members without crowding?

Can furnishings be arranged to give an illusion of space, to carry the eye from one area to another, so that those who might feel confined receive the impression of a wider area of space than that in the particular room?

There will be many different areas for socialization, interaction, and relaxation in the home; a living room, family room, den, patio, study, dining area, and kitchen — each family has its own unique approach, depending in part on the physical space available.

In climates where the outdoors is an important part of the environment of the home, some of this activity may well take place there. The basic concepts for planning for psychological space needs in relation to socialization may be applied and adapted to any area to which people can relate and in which they can be comfortable.

Pets have favorite places in the home, and "lay claim"
to territories just as do other members of the family.
Their needs should be considered, too, in planning areas
for socialization and interaction.
(Courtesy Selig Manufacturing Company and Wall
Covering Industries Bureau. Wallcovering designed by
Jack Lenor Larsen)

The components of these two "front stage" rooms are
similar—a sofa, two comfortable chairs, a desk, and a
unit of easily movable furniture. In one grouping, the
chairs and sofa are in a rather close arrangement—ideal
for contact people who like to "touch" as they talk. In
the other, the same components are spaced further apart.
There's still opportunity for interaction, but more feeling
of personal space for the noncontacts who need this.
(Courtesy J.C. Penney Company, Inc.)

Selecting Furnishings To Encourage Interaction, Socialization, and Conversation. Some people say this is a lost art, others enjoy it. Perhaps care in the selection and arrangement of furnishings would encourage it.

One of the first prerequisites is comfortable seating. A chair must support the back as well as the legs. There is nothing more uncomfortable for a short person than to have to sit in a chair from which his legs cannot reach the floor. To compensate, he will usually sit forward in the chair, thus losing back support. According to Dr. Janet Travell one cannot relax if furniture is uncomfortable.

A well-designed chair provides the right amount of support for the body at the right places and helps keep muscles stretched to their proper tension. If muscles are overstretched from sitting improperly, they fail to keep the ligaments and joints in line, and muscle injury and joint strain can result from sagging of the body.

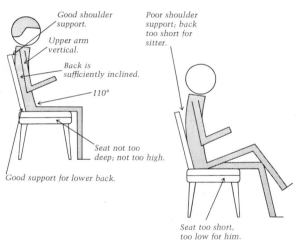

Good shoulder support.

Upper arm vertical.

Back is sufficiently inclined.

110°

Seat not too deep; not too high.

Good support for lower back.

Poor shoulder support; back too short for sitter.

Seat too short, too low for him.

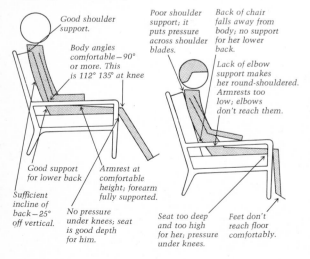

Good shoulder support.

Body angles comfortable—90° or more. This is 112° 135° at knee.

Poor shoulder support; it puts pressure across shoulder blades.

Back of chair falls away from body; no support for her lower back.

Lack of elbow support makes her round-shouldered. Armrests too low; elbows don't reach them.

Good support for lower back.

Armrest at comfortable height; forearm fully supported.

Sufficient incline of back—25° off vertical.

No pressure under knees; seat is good depth for him.

Seat too deep and too high for her; pressure under knees.

Feet don't reach floor comfortably.

Other Considerations for Adequate Support of Body. The ischial and tuberosities bones in the middle of each buttock are intended by nature to support the weight of the upper half of the body, not the muscles. A chair should be designed so that one sits with the weight of the body on the center of the seat, not on the sides of the buttocks.

A chair that provides adequate support for one person may be totally or partially inadequate for another. Developing a sensitivity to the comfort of individuals in an area planned for interaction may be as important as how the furniture is arranged.

Some Features To Check

1. Support for lower back

A chair needs forward roll at the back to give support to the lumbar curve; sitting for a long time without this support can fatigue back muscles and can cause the individual to become tense.

2. Height of armrests

If armrests are too high they push shoulders up and forward creating stiffness and pain across shoulders and back of neck.

Too high armrests.

3. Degree of back scoop should allow shoulder blades to drop back slightly behind the center of the spine at shoulder level

If the back is too scooped it rounds the back, rolls the shoulders forward, and may cause severe muscle strain.

Back too scooped.

4. Slope of back 15 to 20 inches behind the vertical is a comfortable slope

A nearly vertical back (for example, straight ballroom chairs) forces the individual to droop forward into a rounded shoulder position.

5. Height of back needs to support shoulders

If too short, it can give a stiff and aching neck.

Back too short.

6. Comfortable sitting position body should be at 90° angle at waist and at knees to prevent overstretching of back and calf muscles

A chair with too low a seat makes hips sag below the knees and distorts lower back—creating backache.

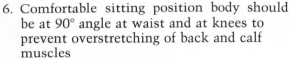

Jack-knifing.

7. Edge of chair

If a hard high edge comes just above the knee, under the thigh, it can exert pressure on the main artery and veins there, disturbing the circulation of the blood to and from the lower part of the legs, causing swelling and pain.

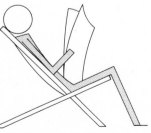

Hard pressure under thighs.

8. Height of chair from seat to floor—this is a personal matter. Legs should touch the floor, not dangle

The average straight chair measures 17 inches from the front of the seat to floor. If legs don't touch the floor, swelling and pain may result.

Sometimes a chair is so well designed that it stands the test of time. The traditional rocking chair is one example.

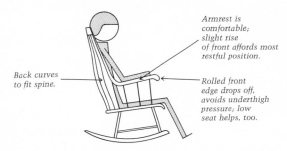

Armrest is comfortable; slight rise of front affords most restful position.

Back curves to fit spine.

Rolled front edge drops off, avoids underthigh pressure; low seat helps, too.

It also favors circulation by alternately relaxing and contracting the muscles, thus preventing stiffness.

Besides adequate seating, other factors that contribute to a relaxed comfortable environment for conversation include having a flat surface (table, dresser top, shelf, trunk top) within easy reach of seating so that objects such as eyeglasses, papers, or food, may be placed there when not in use.

Naturally furniture must be grouped so those conversing can establish eye contact. However, facing a bright light (from a broad expanse of window, for example) can be tiring to the eye if it is exposed for an extended period of time; therefore, the seating arrangement should be planned, so that those sitting will not directly face the light from the window.

Viewing TV. TV can be a positive tool for interaction, as a focus for conversation and entertainment when a group enjoys a particular program together as well as when someone alone becomes involved in a particular program. Comfortable seating should be arranged facing the screen, or should be easy to rearrange to see the screen when desired.

Telephone. The role of the telephone in interaction potential should not be overlooked. It can be a communication bridge to those who do not have immediate family with whom to interact and socialize.

Study or Writing Area. All study areas are not necessarily needed for deep intellectual work. Some may serve as a background for socialization and interaction. The organization of storage of supplies and work surface will need to be planned around the four steps outlined in Chapter 3 to meet unique needs.

Placement for interaction is another matter:
A small desk area tucked into a corner of a room or hall could be within sight and sound of a child at play, encouraging communication between parent and child.

Similarily, a desk in a bedroom shared by two might provide an opportunity for communication when one has work to do and the other may want to read in bed or watch TV.

In a room shared by the entire family, a study area might be planned in a relatively quiet corner; several different activities could be carried on in the room by different family members at the same time; all could know the security of having someone else in the room, without being actively involved with one another.

A dining room, used only on special occasions, can do double duty, nicely, as a "community" study room for several family members. In fact, such an arrangement might inspire those who need help, to relate to another in solving a problem.

This same arrangement could work around the kitchen table, too.

The smell of a crackling fire in the fireplace, the aroma of food cooking nearby and the anticipation of a delicious meal—these can be positive sensory stimulants. (1971 BURLINGTON HOUSE AWARD WINNER "The Nantucket House")

*Although the television set does not dominate this
room, it is placed on a shelf where it can be seen from
most seating in the room. The rocker can be easily
moved to face the screen if desired.
The floor-to-ceiling bookcase was made from eight
foot ladders that were stained, varnished, and nailed to
the wall.
(1971 BURLINGTON HOUSE AWARD WINNER
"Do-It-Yourself Home in Milwaukee")*

In this unusual home the concept of a "kiva" is applied to an area for conversation. The term "kiva" comes from the Pueblo Indians who use it to describe a large area, partly underground, used for religious ceremonies or other purposes. Interaction in the form of conversation surely can qualify for this description.

Here, the fireplace is bordered by a circular vinyl padded built-in bench. The circular seating encourages conversation. Those interacting can maintain eye contact and all can feel part of one group.
(1971 BURLINGTON HOUSE AWARD WINNER "Unusual Dwelling in the Southwest")

Entertainment. One of the outcomes of a party most hostesses deplore, is a natural division of men and women, each sex seated on its "own side" of the room. How can it be avoided?

First, it would be wise to analyze why it happens.

Is it because:

The women are given the most comfortable seating (perhaps the sofa and an adjoining chair) while the men are left with the "hard" chairs which they move to form a grouping of their own?

The furnishings aren't flexible enough to embrace a large group, to be moved aside if necessary, or regrouped easily for socialization involving more than two or three people?

No real plan has been made for the occasion, no conversation starters, or group activity to encourage interaction and involvement?

Seating is not comfortable?

Everyone can't see or be involved in a central entertainment plan? (For example, in showing of home movies, can everyone see the screen?)

So often, in an area for entertainment, whether indoors or out, variations of the stereotype cliche are used for furnishings—one sofa, two end tables, and two matching chairs, with a table in between. Perhaps a new approach, with interaction potential in mind, would eliminate some of the problems.

Dual Purpose Furnishings. Sometimes an area for socialization serves a dual purpose. It may be a part-time guest room, a sewing room, a study area, or a one-room apartment that is an area for socialization, study, and eating during the day and a bedroom by night.

Functional steps of all activities should be carefully planned to insure adequate space for all and to avoid safety hazards. For example, lights should be placed so that a long walk across the room is not necessary to turn lights out before going to bed. This can be especially hazardous for guests who are not familiar with the arrangement of the furniture. It helps also not to have to move too many pieces of furniture in order to open out a sofa bed, for instance.

Relaxation. The dictionary definition of relaxation is "relief of bodily or mental effort." How each person finds this relief is partly a pattern learned within the family, partly an expression of personal interests.

Home might very well be a good place to encourage family members to relax, to find relief from the efforts and pressures of the day. It might even provide opportunities for individuals to experiment to learn what "turns them on"—music, art, a garden, building, refinishing, cooking, needlework, contemplation—there can be no end to such a list.

Why not plan relaxation areas where any member of the family can become involved in an activity, if they want to try it. Or, maybe, set up a study area, with books that encourage research.

In families with a high interest in creative projects, group interaction can range from total participation to involvement in decision making or critique. And it can take place anywhere—in the house—or outdoors—down cellar, or in the kitchen.

A few examples of some creative approaches to planning dual purpose areas are illustrated on the following pages. The possibilities are limitless, depending on the needs and imagination of the people involved.

An entertainment plan in an area can take many different forms. It might be a movie screen that rolls down from behind the window treatment in a tiny room, with the projector for home movies permanently placed on a chest behind the sofa. When the screen is not being used the area can be used for conversation, relaxation, contemplation.
(Courtesy J.C. Penney Company, Inc.)

*Selection of furniture is one of the key factors in plan-
ning for dual purpose rooms.
Milo Baughman in his "New Concept II," collection has
designed flexible furnishings that can be used to create
arrangements for encouraging interaction, in large groups
as well as smaller ones. By rearranging furniture the
area can be changed to meet many different needs.
(Courtesy Thayer Coggin, Inc.)*

In this handsome, round-the-clock room, interior designer Peg Walker used a sofa that doubles as a bed as the decorative focal point. The tailored window shades also serve as room darkeners.

The room was designed with mobility in mind. For example, the twin coffee tables are light and small enough to slip out of the way and stack at night. The Brazilian rosewood book tree also does double duty—it is an interestingly designed vertical storage piece that

keeps reading matter close at hand, and boasts an
illuminated panel that acts as reading light at bedtime.
Window sills and the recesses beneath serve as storage
and TV stand, while the black plastic table on a clear,
sculptured base divides its time between library and
dining duties. An undulating bentwood chair adds
"wing chair" comfort in contemporary style.
(Courtesy Window Shade Manufacturers Association
and Brennen Shades)

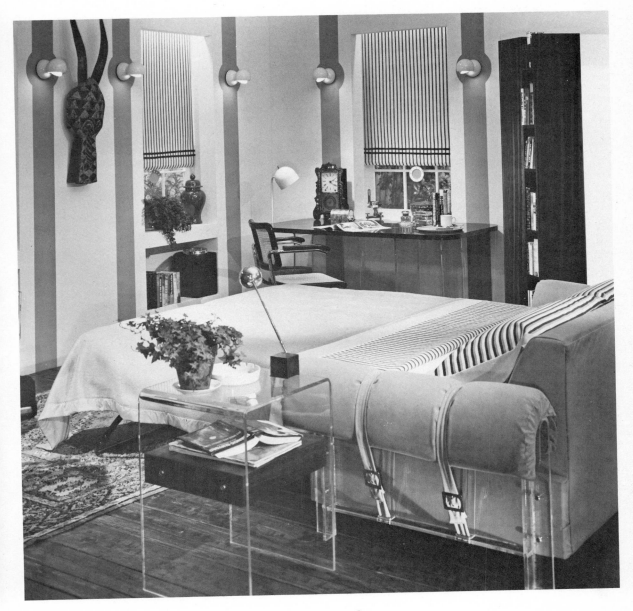

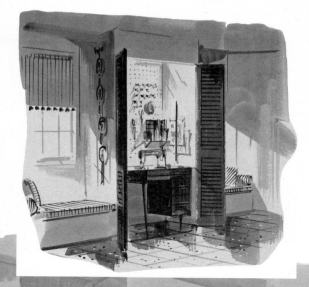

On the facing page, a bedroom-study in an old brownstone is the design of John Hayden, N.S.I.D. The leafy indigo and mocha patterned fabric was laminated to shade cloth. A picnic table was turned into a desk, and the picnic bench, converted to a slim-lined coffee table, runs the entire length of the brass daybed which has been upholstered—and bolstered. Garden chairs create extra seating without taking too much room.
(Courtesy Window Shade Manufacturers Association and Tontine Window Shades)

The dual purpose of a room need not always be obvious, as shown on this page. Sometimes, an area can be built in, which can be closed off when not in use. Here, an enclosed section of this room houses sewing machine and sewing equipment storage above it. The window seats also double as storage units.
(Courtesy J.C. Penney Company, Inc.)

Relationship of Various Activities. Too much activity, literally or figuratively, will not encourage relaxation or socialization.

An illusion of too much busyness may be created by:
Too many furnishings.
Too many things to attract the eye so that it constantly moves from one object to another.
Too many activities planned for one area.
Too many color contrasts.
Too many dominant and "moving" lines in patterns of wallpaper and fabrics used in the area.

All can contribute to fatigue and tension. However, reactions will be very personal. What is a lively design to one individual may very well be busy to another. In a group situation like a family one, a group decision may well be called for in planning furnishings for an area that all will use.

What's really important is how the human relationships will be influenced by activities in the area. If home is to be an environment to which individuals can relate, then obviously it must encourage involvement, not dominate or overpower the very people it is being planned to encourage. In the process of discovering reactions to what is too much activity or design, in a given area, individuals and families may gain insight into their own personal needs. The growing process alone may well be worth the time and effort expended in carefully involving all those who will share the environment in decisions about how various elements alone, and together, influence them. The process may also contribute to understanding of others in the home.

Lighting for Activities. Adequate lighting is as necessary to interaction as the selection and arrangement of furnishings. It can influence the mood of an area as well as provide light for the task. High levels of general lighting make an area seem lively and cheerful and people in it will be more inclined toward activity. Conversely, a feeling of restfulness, relaxation, and intimacy is created when the illumination level is low.

A "soft" or diffused light minimizes shadows while a "hard" light can have much the effect as sunlight, creating highlights and shadows, focusing on particular objects or areas.

Most seeing takes place against a background of light reflected from major surfaces such as walls, draperies, and large pieces of furniture. Therefore, visual comfort, will be influenced by the balance between the sources of illumination, the things to be seen, and the backgrounds against which they are to be viewed.

These are recommendations for reflections for major surfaces:

	Minimum	Maximum
	(In Percent)	
Ceilings		
Pale color tints	60	90
Walls		
Medium shades	35	60
Floors		
Carpeting		
Tiles, woods	15	35

Lighting in a given area can be planned for three purposes — general lighting, functional lighting for the task, and decorative lighting. Often one lighting system serves more than one of these functions. For instance, lighting for a task can contribute to general lighting.

Usually, general lighting balances the lighting in a room—it ties together the lighting provided for visual activities.

Decorative lighting can be used as an element of design in the room.

Although general lighting and light as an element of design are important, the first consideration in planning lighting is visual comfort for the task. To achieve this, the lighting must fulfill two major requirements:

1. Adequate illumination.
2. Suitable luminance (brightness) ratios in the visual field.

The visual field of a person involved in a task will have three zones:

1. The task.
2. Area immediately surrounding the task.
3. General surroundings.

The brightness ratio in all three areas is important. If the relationships aren't balanced, the individual can experience distraction, fatigue, and difficulty in seeing.

Extreme contrasts in light cause fatigue if the eye must adjust back and forth from one to the other.

The position of the light source and the size and shape of the shades also influence the amount and quality of light available for a particular activity.

If the light bulb is high in the shade there will not be as much light on the work area as there will be if the bulb is placed nearer the bottom edge of the shade.

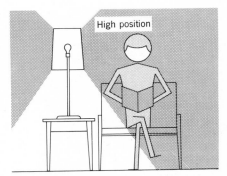

High position

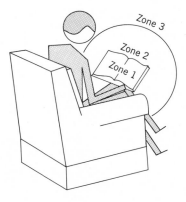

Zone 3
Zone 2
Zone 1

Low position

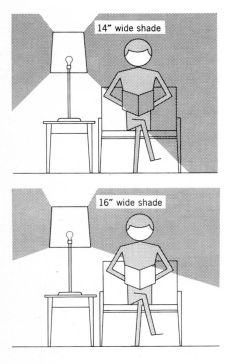

14" wide shade

16" wide shade

Deep narrow shades restrict the spread of light both up and down.

For better reflectance, it also helps if the inner surface of the shade is white or off white. A pleasing effect is usually achieved when white or light shades are used against light walls, and dark shades against darker walls.

Opaque shades can be visually uncomfortable, due to pools of light that are created above and below the shade, unless there are other light sources in the room.

Dark colors and surfaces absorb light so that if the light source is dependent on reflective light, the surrounding surfaces (walls, rugs, lamp shades) should be light colored.

Once the specific lighting for activities is determined, general lighting can then be planned to unify the area.

The amount of lighting recommended for tasks is specified by the lighting engineers in units called footcandles. A footcandle is the amount of light on a surface one foot from a candle.

Minimum recommendations for footcandles for general lighting are:

Conversation, relaxation, entertainment 10
Passage areas for safety 10

Some minimum footcandle recommendations for specific tasks are:

Dining	15 (16)
Grooming, shaving, makeup	50 (54)
Handcraft	
Ordinary seeing tasks	70 (75)
Difficult seeing tasks	100 (110)
Very difficult seeing tasks	150 (160)
Critical seeing tasks	200 (220)
Ironing (hand and machine)	50 (54)
Kitchen duties	
Food preparation and cleaning (at sink, range and counter) involving difficult seeing tasks	150 (160)
Serving and other noncritical tasks	50 (54)
Laundry tasks	
Preparation, sorting, inspection	50 (54)
Tub area-soaking, tinting, hand wash	50 (54)
Washer and dryer areas	30 (32)
Reading and writing	
Handwriting, reproductions, and poor copies	70 (75)
Books, magazines, and newspapers	30 (32)
Reading piano or organ scores	
Advanced (substandard size)	150 (160)
Advanced	70 (75)
Simple	30 (32)
Sewing	
Hand (dark fabrics)	200 (220)
Hand (medium fabrics)	100 (110)

Hand (light fabrics)	50 (54)
Hand (occasional high contrast)	30 (32)
Sewing	
Machine (dark fabrics)	200 (220)
Machine (medium fabrics)	100 (110)
Machine (light fabrics)	50 (54)
Machine (occasional-high contrast)	30 (32)
Study	70 (75)
Table games	30 (32)
Table tennis	20 (22)

These recommendations by the Illuminating Engineering Society are based on the needs of young eyes with 20–20 vision. Older persons or those with sight problems may need more light and special precautions against glare.

The position of the source of light and the amount of light in the bulbs will total up to the required footcandles.

To translate footcandles into practical terms, it is important to understand another lighting term — lumen. A lumen is the unit of light quantity produced by a light source. One lumen per square foot equals one footcandle. As of January 1971, an FTC ruling requires that all packages of household-type bulbs list wattage, lumen, and the average life of bulbs.

Some general lumen recommendations per square foot are:

Living room	80	Bedroom	70
Dining room	45	Hallway	45
Kitchen	80	Laundry	70
Bathroom	65	Workbench area	70

These are recommended lumens when portable lamps, surface-mounted fixtures, and structural lighting techniques are used. These figures should be approximately doubled when a high percentage of the room lighting comes from recessed equipment.

Lamp Placement for Reading with Shade Above Eye Level

Lamp Placement for Reading with Shade at Eye Level

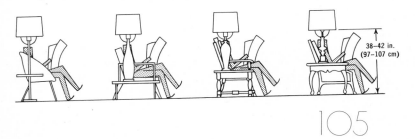
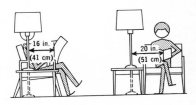

Lamp Placement for Reading with Shade Above Eye Level

When floor lamp height to lower edge of shade or lamp-base-plus-table height is above eye level of 42–49 inches (107–125 cm) right or left rear corner of the lamp should be placed close to the chair. This is possible only when chairs or sofas are at least 10 to 12 inches (25–31 cm) from the wall.

Lamp Placement for Reading with Shade at Eye Level

Average seated eye level is 38–42 inches (97–107 cm) above floor. Lower edge of floor or table lampshades should be at eye level when the lamp is beside the user. This is the correct placement for most table lamps, and for floor lamps serving furniture placed against a wall. Floor lamps with built-on tables should have shades no higher than eye level.

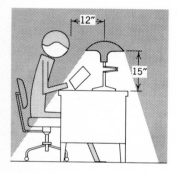

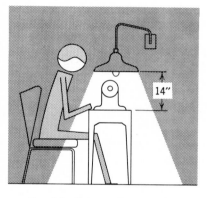

For Desk Work. Lamp placement is very important so that shadows from the individual's hand will not be cast on the work. It should be used with other light in the room. The desk surface should be light in color (30–50% reflectance) and the surface should not be glossy.

For Machine Sewing. Because of similarity in the color of thread and fabric, machine sewing can be visually difficult. This will depend in part, of course, on the reflectance of the materials being used and the amount of contrast. Equipment should be placed so that shadows by the hands of the person sewing are not cast on the work.

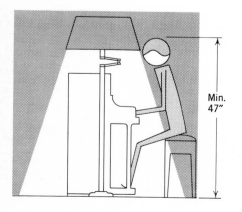

For Music. Luminance can best be controlled if the player faces a wall. Care must be exercised to prevent glare to other persons in the room, as well as to the person reading the music.

For Hand Sewing. Light source should be opposite the hand being used to eliminate shadows on the task.

For Games. The lighting requirements will, of course, vary with the game.

Some general considerations include:

If the game uses a ball, there should be enough contrast with the background surfaces so the player can see the ball.

Uneven distribution of light can make the ball seem to move faster or slower as it passes in and out from areas of greater illumination to lower illumination.

For Hobbies. If performed at a table or workbench:

The wall immediately behind it should have a reflectance of, at least, 40 percent. This will provide good illumination as well as eye comfort.

General lighting should also be provided to prevent sharp contrasts from the lighted area of the task to the surroundings.

Eyes should be shielded from direct daylight glare by use of window blinds or shades.

The image of the light source should not be reflected in glossy materials that might be in use.

For Lighting Accessories. Lighting accents objects and brings colors to life, as well as creating interest by an interplay of light and shadow.

For Viewing TV. Background lighting of some kind is desirable so that there will not be a sharp contrast between the screen and other areas in the room. Sharp contrasts can cause eye fatigue.

Lighting Paintings and Wall Hangings. Lighting equipment should be placed so that the light rays hit the center from an angle of 30 degrees with the vertical to prevent reflections from the surface to the viewer's eyes. There should be general lighting also to avoid a sharp contrast between the object being lighted and the surroundings.

Sculpture. Since this is three dimensional, many exciting effects are possible, both with diffused light and direct lighting. Down lighting can also create visual drama, as with the lighting of metal sculpture in an outdoor garden.

Glass objects may be effectively lighted from below.

Plants. Interesting texture shadow effects are possible with carefully planned lighting. Front lighting of leaves can emphasize color and texture; back lighting may reveal leaf structure; "grazing" a surface with light (such as the trunk of a tree) will emphasize its texture; a low-voltage spotlight beamed on a leaf can create interesting shadows.

The illustrations below and on the following pages demonstrate how lighting can be used to light paintings, sculpture, glass objects, and plants. (Courtesy Large Lamp Department, General Electric Company)

SOURCES OF INFORMATION

Boger, Louise Ade, *Furniture Past and Present*, Doubleday and Company, New York, N.Y., 1966.

Brofenbrenner, Urie, "Who Makes The Generation Gap?" Penney's *Forum*, Spring and Summer 1968.

"Design Criteria for Lighting Interior Living Spaces," prepared by the Residence Lighting Committee of The Illuminating Engineering Society as a recommended practice.

Illuminating Engineering Society
345 East 47th Street
New York, N.Y. 10017

Duvall, Evelyn Millis, "High School Girls and the Tasks of Homemaking," Research Finds, *Marriage and Family Living*, November 1960.

Fromm, Erich, *The Art of Loving*, New York, Basic Books, Inc., 1963, p. 43.

Hook, Nancy C., and Paolucci, Beatrice, "The Family as an Ecosystem," *Journal of Home Economics* Vol. 62, No. 5, May 1970, pp. 315–318.

Gaylin, Ned L., "New Uses for the Family Room," a presentation at Michigan State University, Colloquy on the Family, East Lansing, Michigan, April 9, 1970.

General Electric Lighting Institute, Nela Park, Cleveland, Ohio

Lane, Betty, "Attitudes of Youth Toward the Aged," *Journal of Marriage and the Family*, May 1964, pp. 229–231.

Lynn, David B., "Learning Masculine and Feminine Roles," *Marriage and Family Living*, February 1963.

Lynn, David B., "The Husband-Father Role in the Family," *Marriage and Family Living*, Vol. XXIII, Aug. 1961.

McCullough, K. P., Smith, R. H., Wood, A. L., Woolrich, A., "Space Standards for Household Activities," *Bulletin 686*. University of Illinois Agricultural Experiment Station.

Montgomery, James, E., "Impact of Housing Patterns on Marital Interaction," *The Family Coordinator* July 1970, pp. 267–274.

Meehan, Elizabeth, Color and Lighting Design Coordinator, Sylvania Electric Products, Inc., Danvers, Mass.

Otto, Herbert, "What Is A Strong Family?" *Marriage and Family Living*, Vol. XXIV, No. 1, February 1962.

Smith, Downer, and Lynch, "The Man in the House," *The Family Coordinator* April 1969, pp. 107–110.

Travell, Janet, M.D., "Chairs are a Personal Thing," *House Beautiful*, October 1955.

Watts, Joanne, *The Women's Guide to the Orient*, Published by Japan Air Lines, 1970.

Area for Food Preparation

Perhaps one of the most tradition-bound rooms in the home is the kitchen. For generations it has been the area associated with the bustle of preparing meals and the aroma of cooking food. Somehow, too, more attention has been given to helping families plan efficient and attractive kitchens than to most other rooms. Maybe this is as it should be. After all, based on three meals a day, a total of 1095 meals could be prepared in one year.

But with living patterns changing, and technology bringing new innovations in rapid succession to everyday living, it might be a good time to pause and consider:

Why is food preparation always centered in the kitchen?
Could food be prepared at the point where it will be consumed?

Out of the imagination stage and even beyond the drawing board, right now there are prototypes of equipment for food preparation that could be used to fulfill unique needs throughout the home.

Cold storage for food can be provided by small modular units built into the walls of homes. These mini refrigerators can be placed inconspicuously at points of key use — bedroom, study, laundry, living area, and nursery — wherever cold food and beverages might be needed. These units work silently, fed by cool air that is channeled throughout hidden ducts connected to a compact, central cooling unit. Small units for heating food may also be similarly located at key points.
Sequential modules, a new breed of appliances, can do double and triple duty. For example, the tasks of setting the table and

*This combination table, dishwasher, and storage
sequential module has been designed for the Whirlpool
Kitchen of the Future.*
*Cooking elements, sink and counters are concealed in
back of the wall paneling. The strip of mirrors is actually
a series of doors to eye-level refrigerator, freezer, oven
and storage space.*
(Courtesy Whirlpool Corporation)

later clearing it of soiled dishes can be combined in one unit that is a combination dining table, dishwasher, and storage unit. The unit will have a center section that elevates to accept soiled dishes. After the washing cycle is completed, the built-in washer acts as a storage area for the dishes. Why not one dishwasher near the area where major baking and cooking will be done — for pots and pans — and another in the dining area to wash and store dishes for eating?

Another sequential module already conceived is a portable refrigerator-oven. It operates on a thermoelectric principle whereby two metals that are dissimilar, such as copper and bismuth, are used to conduct electrical current. When positive polarity is used, heat will be produced. Reversing the polarity of the current will produce cold. Thus, a roast, a casserole, and the like could be stored under refrigeration until needed. Then, the turn of a switch or an automatic timer could alter the current and the unit would become an oven, heating the stored food, perhaps right in the area where it will be eaten.

Still another possibility, now well beyond the drawing board stage, is a microwave oven that incorporates a freezer. With the pressing of a button, the contents from the freezer are transferred to the oven where they can be cooked in minutes.

Computers play no small role, too, in the potential for decentralizing food preparation in the home. They can be programmed to set food preparation devices into operation when special buttons are pressed, resulting in a complete meal. They may even be activated by a telephone call. Also the computer can give a complete inventory readout of remaining foods and liquids.

The impact of technology is just beginning to be felt; the possibilities for using it to create a meaningful environment in the home are only now beginning to emerge. Of course, food preparation can be more than just a mechanical function in the home. In many families it helps fulfill emotional needs and provides the setting for socializing experiences as well. It can be the activity through which some family members fill their needs for recognition and esteem, for self-confidence, and even the need for belonging. Others may find food preparation a creative experience, a step toward self-expression and self-actualization. And for some, the preparation of food may be a way of expressing love.

In deciding the relative importance of food preparation in the family value structure, these questions might be considered:

How important is mealtime in the family?
Is it a regularly structured activity in the home? If so, how often? Where? Do all family members participate?
Do individuals eat at their convenience? How often? Where?
What other activities take place during food-preparation time?
Is it also the time when some family members relate together?
Is this the time of day, perhaps, when the mother and one or more of the children can be together for conversation as well as work? Or when husband and wife exchange news of the day, perhaps, while they prepare the meal and relax from work, or while they do the dishes after the meal? Or,

Portable Thermoelectric Refrigerator in the Whirlpool Kitchen of the Future pops out from wall with the push of a button and can be rolled anywhere. It keeps food chilled, then, with the flip of a switch, becomes an oven.

if there is an older member of the family, is this a time for all three generations to be together in a common activity?

Are there intangible factors?
Are there steps in the preparation of a meal that are used as a vehicle to give some family members an opportunity to gain recognition (and, perhaps, self-confidence, too) — to feel needed and wanted?
Is it an activity with built-in opportunities to teach some family members to assume responsibility and to face up to the consequences if they do not carry out their tasks? Does it provide the opportunity to learn the importance of timing and coordination of efforts?

The intangible role of fulfilling human needs other than the basic one of hunger may be one of the reasons why the kitchen has been a fairly traditional room in the home. In the early days of the Pilgrims, the open hearth at the end of the room, with its kettles and skillets, served not only as the area for food preparation and eating but it also provided warmth and light — a natural place for the family to gather, to relate, and to communicate.

In Amish homes, even today, the kitchen is the center of activity during the week, since the rest of the first floor is closed off, for use only on weekends for worship services. One end of the kitchen is for food preparation and eating; the other has a bench, chairs, and a small table with a lamp and Bible on it, for family activities. Mealtimes are at exact specified times each day and all family members are expected to stop what they are doing to eat together, each sitting in his special place at the table.

In other times and other cultures the kitchen has been purely an area of function. In fact, in some Polynesian cultures, food preparation is carried out in a separate enclosure, away from the main "house."

The traditions of the kitchen have a history of meeting human needs. Whether this tradition is perpetuated or abandoned for newer approaches to food preparation is a question each family must decide individually. If a traditional area provides a meaningful environment for socialization, for the expression of family values and life-style, who can dispute its importance? After all, change for the sake of change alone, is meaningless.

But one must be honest in searching for answers. It's all too easy to be complacent — to furnish an area for food preparation the way it's always been done. Or, conversely, to drop all current patterns and try an entirely new approach. Family living patterns can be changed and, sometimes, maybe they should be changed. Only a thorough understanding of the present living patterns and a plan for alternate ways to fulfill the needs now serviced by this area can insure success in human terms. This must include an analysis of current family food preparation patterns, with questions such as:

Whose responsibility is food preparation?
How many family members participate in food preparation? How many enjoy it as a creative outlet?
How many meals a day are prepared at home?
How much time is available for the preparation of meals?
Will some food preparation be done by working members of the family after they come home from work? How much?

119

Is the family a growing one, with children? Or does it include adults only?

Does the family like simple foods, or is there a preference for gourmet foods?

Will there be entertainment of guests for meals? How often? At formal meals? Informal parties? What kinds of foods will be served? Elaborate? Simple? Home cooked? Store purchased?

How much space for food preparation is available in the home?

What food preparation and storage facilities are available?

Which facilities are desirable and needed?

How often is shopping done for food?

Arrangement of Furnishings

Function, of course, is the prime factor to be considered in planning the arrangement of furnishings for food preparation. Storage of "tools" to do the job is an important part of this function also. A step-by-step analysis of each activity in this area (see page 36) must precede any plans for the arrangement of furnishings. There are three or four major work areas related to food preparation.

Sink Area. This area really serves a dual purpose—it is important in food preparation and in the cleanup after meals. Ideally, the foods that need to be washed, soaked, or peeled before use should be stored in this area. So, too, should:

The pans that might need to be filled with water for cooking.

The coffee pot, coffee, and measuring spoon.

Utensils such as knives, measuring equipment, and stirring spoons that might be used here.

The cleaning supplies for dishes and sink.

Food waste disposal.

A dishwasher, if this is practical for the family. This unit will require the following space:

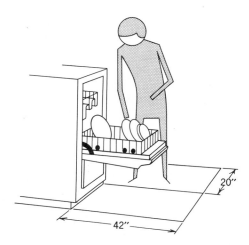

A front-opening dishwasher requires 4 inches more space than using other appliances in a kitchen

Some kind of space on either side of a sink is desirable—24 inches of working space on each side is considered minimum. A cutting board designed to fit over the sink can make it easy to collect parings for disposal.

Alternate Ideas. A food-preparation area may have more than one sink center—perhaps, an island for the preparation of foods and another for the cleaning of pots and pans and the preparations for cooking. In a decentralized plan, mini-sinks may be located in different

The sink area in this kitchen is organized for function, with supplies and utensils within easy reach. (Reprinted by special permission of LADIES' HOME JOURNAL © Downe Publishing, Inc.)

areas of the home, adjacent to individual refrigeration or baking units.

Range Area. Cooking, of course, is the prime function here. Baking may be, too, if the oven and range are one unit. Some small appliances, such as a blender, an electric can opener, as well as pots and baking trays, may be located in this area.

Room may be needed on either side of the range to maneuver pots and pans, and around the oven to place units being removed from it. Room may be needed also for foods placed in serving dishes if they are to be taken to another room, or for dishes, if food is served from the cooking source onto the plates.

Storage in this area can be personalized to meet the needs of individual work patterns.

If oven and range must be near each other, it's best to allow some counter space in between for cooking and baking pans when they are removed from the heat source.

Ovens installed in corners can be awkward, for loading and unloading, as well as cleaning. Minimum physical space requirements in this area are:

Door should be 2″ below the elbow of the person using the oven the most.

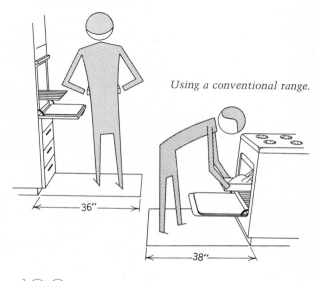

Using a conventional range.

123

Individual expression can be combined with function to create an interesting and useful food preparation environment.
Suspended from a beautifully carved molding over the range in this kitchen, the bright orange and copper pots are colorful as well as convenient for use. A large collection of earthenware cooking containers, and a generous supply of mixing spoons are also placed within easy reach.
(1971 BURLINGTON HOUSE AWARD WINNER "The Ski House." Photo Courtesy House Beautiful, © 1970 Hearst Corporation)

Opposite page:
Both the microwave oven in the corner and the regular range and oven in this kitchen have been designed with flat surfaces on either side. The combination refrigerator-freezer is also placed near flat surfaces. Note storage for wine above refrigerator-freezer unit.
(Courtesy Wood-Mode Cabinetry)

Alternate Ideas. A microwave oven-freezer appliance could be placed near the dining area, and activated from another area in the home, so that food preparation in the final consumption stage is one step.
Simple meals might be prepared in different areas of the home:

A mobile food cart could hold all the ingredients for a meal as well as the appliance in which to cook. In fact, the cart could be organized to hold all utensils (including dishes) for eating, as well as cooking, with room for dirty dishes and leftover scraps as well.

Or, a single-purpose appliance — electric frying pan, broiler, or casserole — can be used at point of need (alone or in concert with other appliances) to make a meal.

Active families, with interests that vary, may find this type of arrangement suitable for the enjoyment of world series games on television, a cool breeze under a tree on a warm day, a sunset, or a special activity outdoors.

Refrigerator Center. Not only is this the area for storage of some foods but logically it can be adjacent to the mix area, since many supplies for baking are taken from the refrigerator. Adequate counter space (at least 15 inches) on the opening side of the refrigerator will allow room for groceries to be put away, as well as for the removal of food and supplies. Some centers include a freezer as part of the unit, or as a second appliance in the area.

If a refrigerator, which generates cold, must be placed next to a dishwasher or range (which generates heat) a minimum 3-inch space as well as an insulated strip will add longer life to both appliances.

This portable cart is practically a mobile refreshment center. It includes two cubic feet of refrigerator space, coffee maker, toaster, clock radio, tape cartridge player and additional storage space.
(Courtesy Philco-Ford Corporation)

When planning the area, the following considerations are important:

The door of the refrigerator should open away from a counter or work area for easy removal of foods.

Doors coming into the food preparation area should be hinged so that they do not open against the door of the refrigerator (or other appliance, for that matter)

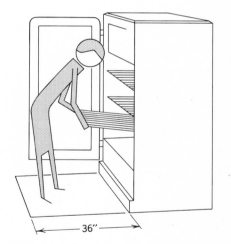

At least 36 inches is needed for opening the door and removing foods from the refrigerator.

Alternatives. Small refrigerators have been around for a long time. They are standard furnishings in some offices, as well as in tiny kitchens of apartments. But, the concept of many small refrigerators throughout the home, to supplement a large one, perhaps, for main storage of foods, is slow to take hold.

Why not a refrigerator in the bedroom for midnight snacks, along with a percolator or small appliance for heating foods?

Or a refrigerator could be located in the play area (perhaps, this is the basement of the home) for soft drinks and fruits; one could also be in a study or just next to the door to the outdoors, to quench thirsts on a warm day.

Eating Area. A place to eat might very well be part of this area. Basic considerations have been outlined in the next chapter.

Other thoughts include:

A counter nearby to hold dirty dishes or foods to be served.

A direct light source at the table may be necessary, either in the form of candles or an overhead light.

A table or eating area should be out of the traffic path.

A mobile cart to keep foods warm that organizes all components needed for the meal, and saves time in clearing the table can be convenient.

Relationship of Various Activities to One Another

Activity in a traditional food preparation area is usually concentrated between three areas—the sink, refrigerator, and range. If a pattern of the steps taken between these areas were made, a triangle would probably be developed for most efficient placement. In order to space these centers for convenience, some minimum measurements are:

The total triangle from center to center should be over 13 feet and less than 22 feet with no single arm of that triangle measuring less than 4 feet 6 inches. The triangle should be arranged to keep casual traffic from crossing the work triangle.

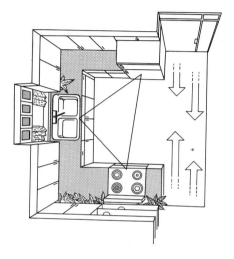

Furthermore, certain minimum physical requirements for working space in this area include:

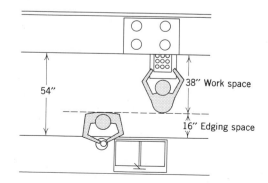

Minimum space (allowing for edging) for two people working at cabinets and appliances opposite each other.

This area for eating is separated from the food prepara-
tion area by a counter that doubles as a serving unit.
Note direct light source over table.
(Reprinted by special permission of LADIES' HOME
JOURNAL © Downe Publishing, Inc.)

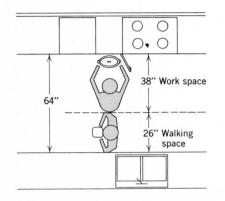

Liberal space (allowing for walking) for two people working at cabinets and appliances opposite each other.

38" Work space

64"

26" Walking space

Using a base cabinet

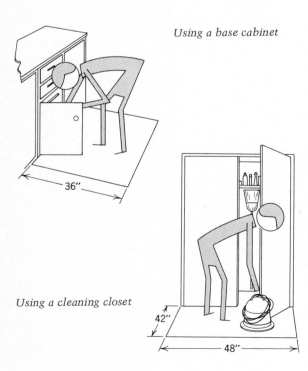

36"

Using a cleaning closet

42"

48"

The sink, refrigerator, and range may already be in place, and it may be impossible to move them. In this case, decisions regarding the arrangement of furnishings must be made to make the best of what may not be an ideal situation.

If, however, it is possible to start "at the beginning," these factors may influence the arrangement of furnishings within the triangle.

The sink area, perhaps, relates to more activities in food preparation than does any other, so it needs to be within easy distance of the refrigerator, range, oven, and mix center.

Trips between the range and sink are probably more frequent than between any other centers in the food preparation area, so they should be close to each other. If a great deal of baking is done, it is also important to place the mix area near the sink. After determining the important activity centers between which an outstanding number of trips are made, it is then best to consider placing together the centers that are used together for various activities.

For example,

The sink and refrigerator centers.
The sink center or dishwasher and the center for storage of dishes.
The range and mix centers (when much baking is done)
The range center and center for storage of dishes.
The dish storage and dining centers.

These represent centers between which there might be much traffic in the course of

130

All supplies and equipment are stored together in this mix center. It utilizes the entire space from counter top to ceiling, is adjacent to sink area and not far from the range.
(Reprinted by special permission of LADIES' HOME JOURNAL © 1970 Downe Publishing, Inc. Photographs by Jerry Abramovitz)

This storage area for dishes placed above the dishwasher makes maximum use of space from counter top to ceiling. The doors have easy-to-clean surfaces. (Reprinted by special permission of LADIES' HOME JOURNAL © Downe Publishing, Inc. Photographs by Jerry Abramovitz)

carrying out activities. Personal work and traffic patterns, however, must be the final determining factors.*

In planning for washing and storage of dishes, these factors should be considered:

Where are soiled dishes first placed when brought from the dining table to the sink center?

Is the counter to the right or left of the sink or, is the sink bowl used?

For example, if used dishes are brought from the table to the sink at the left counter, rinsed and stacked on the right counter, then it might be logical to place the dining center to the left of the sink, rather than the right.

As dishes and utensils are washed, are they placed to the left or right of the sink bowl? If work moves from right to left, the storage center for dishes might be to the left of the sink for the continuous routing of work.

Ideally, the center for storage of dishes should be near the point where they are washed and dried (or removed from the dishwasher) and within a few steps of the dining area, whether it is in the food preparation area or in a separate room. If this is not possible, a decision must be made, based on personal or family preference, to place the center either near the cleaning area or near the dining area.

Some basic kitchen shapes that have been worked out for efficiency include:

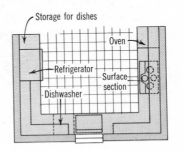

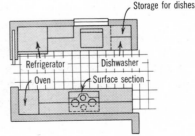

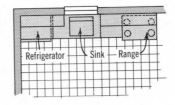

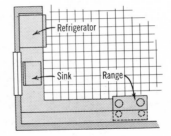

* Rose E. Steidl and Esther Crew Bratten, *Work in the Home*, John Wiley and Sons, New York, 1968, pp. 265–328.

Dish storage planned for an area that serves as a divider between food preparation and eating areas can be convenient to both table and dishwasher as in this kitchen. (Courtesy of "Kitchens by Coppes-Napanee, Nappanee, Indiana")

A Word About Safety

The food preparation area, perhaps more than any other in the average home, has a great potential for accidents.

Developing an awareness for safety in planning this area can prevent accidents. This will involve thinking through the traffic patterns involved in carrying out activities in the area, as well as the details of how appliances and equipment are used and where they are stored. Some of the common hazards are:

Range installed at the end of a line of cabinets in a busy area. Pot and pan handles can protrude into the aisle resulting in painful accidents from both spilling and bumping. Also, in this arrangement, there is no flat surface next to the end of the range. If something should boil over, there is no handy surface nearby to which the pot can be quickly removed, without spilling over the other units.

Sink too close to the range or oven can lead to painful burns and scalds.

Open appliance doors that can block a traffic aisle lead to bruised shins, spilled sauces, and frayed tempers. Also, a narrow aisle in a kitchen invites accidents. Minimum aisle space should be 48 inches.

Fluorescent lights (deluxe warm white) usually mounted under wall cabinets are recommended. They should fill at least 2/3 of the counter length. The lumens used here will depend on the size of the area.
(Courtesy General Electric Company, Large Lamp Department)

Lighting Needs. Some examples of lighting appropriate for various activities in the food preparation area are shown here and on the following two pages. Good lighting can make a difference in how one feels while working in this area. Shadows, glare, and dark spots can create a feeling of fatigue. The amount and kind of lighting used will depend on what activities will be carried on here. In all lighting it is well to remember that the major surfaces in any area form the background against which seeing takes place, whether or not the individual is aware of it. As a result, visual comfort, mental attitude and emotional mood can be influenced by the balance between the things to be seen and the background against which they are seen.

The recommended lumens per square foot for a kitchen are 80. In a room 12×12 feet, this would amount to 11,520 lumens. In planning the distribution of these lumens, specific tasks must be considered.

Food preparation tasks are easier to see when the light over the work surfaces is shadow free. The light source should be well above the cooking utensils to direct light into them when food in preparation needs to be watched.

Some general wattage guidelines are a 30-watt deluxe warm white fluorescent behind a faceboard or one 100-watt or two 60-watt bulbs located in the exhaust hood.

If ironing is to be done in the kitchen, a light source which can be directed toward the task is important to reveal wrinkles. If the light is used above and in front of the person ironing, the shadows will fall toward that person, making it easier to see the wrinkles. Besides this task lighting, general room

Channels of light above the cupboards illuminate the area when doors are open. Counter tops are lighted to eliminate shadows.
(Courtesy General Electric Company, Large Lamp Department)

Lighting can contribute to the beauty as well as the function of an area. In this food preparation area, shadow box lighting above the windows provides a cozy atmoshpere. The pull down lamp over the table, which would use a minimum of 120 watts provides enough light for eating, as well as directing light upward for a pleasing effect.
(Courtesy Large Lamp Department, General Electric Company)

Opposite page:
A fully lighted ceiling banishes all shadows, highlights cabinets, and kitchen fixtures. It creates a stimulating work atmosphere, but is not conducive to relaxation.
(Courtesy General Electric Company)

lighting will also be important to prevent eye fatigue from sharp contrasts.

Wattage of bulbs, incidentally, does not determine brightness. Wattage measures the amount of electricity going into the bulb — it measures the input not the output. It's the lumens that measure the actual output of a bulb, — the amount of brightness produced by the bulb.

Light bulb jackets now indicate watts, lumens, and bulb life. Some bulbs are described as longer life bulbs. They are designed to last longer than standard bulbs, but for bulbs with the same wattage, longer life means less light. The filament in a bulb burns out after a certain amount of use. "Long life" filaments are heavier than those for standard bulbs, so they last longer, but they don't give as much light.

Psychological Space Needs. Many studies have been done about the physical space needs for food preparation. Plans have been developed to provide maximum efficiency and minimum use of energy.

But not much is known about the psychological needs for space. Applying the knowledge developed by Dr. Hall, we can generalize as follows.

Contact persons might welcome a food preparation area that invites participation by members of the family, especially if the area is not too large so that it does not, in essence, become individual work areas. A work area adjacent to a dining or family activity area can keep a "contact" person in touch with the family during a meal, even when some dishes need to be removed from the table, or additional food must be brought to the table.

In fact, an open food preparation area adjacent to living and other activity areas might be quite welcome.

A noncontact family might prefer a rather small area for food preparation which does not permit room for more than one person at a time to work. It might, too, be separate from the dining area and other activity areas. Or, if two people enjoy preparing meals, a very large food preparation area could be arranged to permit separate spaces in which each could work.

In many families, not only is food preparation carried on in the kitchen but this room is also traditionally the "territory" of the woman of the family. In fact, in many cultures the concept of territoriality in relation to the homemaker and her kitchen is an accepted idea — one that is respected by other members of the family. She is the one who decides how it will be arranged, and its equipment is placed to be convenient and efficient for her work patterns. Perhaps the only others permitted to stake out territory in the area are a family pet or one special member of the household.

With food consumption now more readily enjoyed in different areas of the home, and the decentralization of food preparation from the kitchen a real possibility, tomorrow's homemaker may well need to center her emotional need for territoriality in some other activity or area of the home.

The growing interest in food preparation as a creative expression by men as well as women will also have an effect on the concept of the kitchen as the "territory" of the woman of the family. Baking bread, and cooking gourmet foods have become hobbies that various family members now enjoy.

140

Whether one is a contact or noncontact person, an opportunity for socialization and interaction while food is being prepared might be important. One creative approach to providing this opportunity uses a painted plywood panel with cut out for visual contact, which defines the food preparation area, and eating area without separating them completely from the socialization area.
(1971 BURLINGTON HOUSE AWARD WINNER. Photo Courtesy of Glamour Magazine, © 1970 Conde Nast Publications)

A spacious area like this kitchen with its cathedral ceiling and wide expanse of window, can well accommodate the space bubbles of several individuals who might want to create and cook. The center table is a butcher block.
(1972 Burlington House Award, "Man's Home in Washington")

As the number of working women increases, the food preparation area may also have less significance as the territory of the woman in the family and instead, become another activity area where many family members individually or together prepare meals. In time, a trend like this should influence the size and design of the traditional kitchen built into the home, whether it is an apartment or a house.

SOURCES OF INFORMATION

General Electric Company, Large Lamp Division, Nela Park, Cleveland, Ohio.

Hotpoint Kitchen/Laundry Planning Guide and Idea Book, published by General Electric Company, Louisville, Kentucky.

Information about the Amish supplied by Mrs. John J. Herr, Mount Joy, Pennsylvania.

McCullough, K. P., Smith, R. H., Wood, A. L., and Woolrich, A., "Space Standards for Household Activities," Bulletin 686, University of Illinois Agricultural Experiment Station.

Steidl, Rose E., and Bratten, Esther Crew, *Work in the Home*, John Wiley and Sons, New York, 1968, pp. 265–328.

THE FACTS OF LIGHT, Better Light Better Sight Bureau.

Whirlpool Corporation, Benton Harbor, Michigan.

Area for Eating

A place to eat can be almost as personal as a place to rest. Where it is located in the home may be influenced as much by personal values as it is by space limitations. For some, eating may be one of those necessary functions one must perform to replenish energy for more interesting activities; for others, dining may be a pleasure, an opportunity to communicate with the family, the time of day to "unwind" from the day's activities. A place to eat may be almost anywhere in the home; in the kitchen, family room, dining room, one end of the living room, patio, or a tray table in a favorite spot, inside or outside.

To an extent it depends on the degree of influence of the cultural heritage of the family as well as the practical considerations of function, because how one eats may influence when and where one eats. Ideas about how to eat may be acquired by families in their travels as well as from the influence of their cultural background.

Oriental Influences. For the Japanese, food is an esthetic experience. How it is arranged and the appropriateness in design of the dishes on which it is served definitely contribute to the enjoyment of the meal. So does the fellowship in dining, which is considered of equal importance. In traditional Japanese homes, meals are eaten at a low table, with individuals sitting on cushions on the floor. Some families in Japan today are substituting a western type table and chairs.

The Chinese in Taiwan sit on stools around a round table to eat. Mealtime is the best time for the entire family to get together, especially in farm families where they work from sunrise to sunset.

The Chinese consider eating life's greatest and most serious pleasure. They feel that the enjoyment of food is heightened if you first keenly anticipate it and discuss it and then comment after eating it.

The Koreans, on the other hand, discourage conversation at meals. When entertaining, the Chinese hostess does not sit down at the table to eat with her guests. She stays in the kitchen to prepare the food, since it is cooked and served one dish at a time—*hot.* A simple meal will consist of five dishes, a more elaborate meal will have 12 to 16 or more dishes.

European Influences. Mealtime for Europeans is a time for conversation and fellowship, too. Eating with the eyes is as important as the actual consumption of food. The French are especially known for foods that have "eye" appeal as well as appetite appeal, and for the relaxed atmosphere of enjoying the meal.

The Scandinavians are perhaps best known for their influence on how families entertain. The smorgasbord—which literally means a "sandwich board" or table of appetizers to eat before dinner—originated when the Vikings came home from their voyages with foods from other parts of the world. Because there was not enough of all foods for everyone to have a whole meal, the smorgasbord was developed to give everyone, at least, a taste. This type of meal is planned for individuals to go back to the table two and three times, since mixing all the flavors will not enhance the meal. It also means there must be space for the "board" as well as a place to eat.

Early American Traditions. The Pennsylvania Dutch farmer, who was hungry when he came in from the fields wanted all his food for the entire meal placed on the table at one time. Since the meal could not be served elaborately by courses, the homemaker compensated by baking foods in fancy shapes to make

them look attractive. Traditionally, too, she served "seven sweets and seven sours" to add to the variety and interest of the table.

In the early New England days, the kitchen or "keeping room" was the place where the family ate as well as carried out other activities around the warmth of the hearth. The tradition of old-fashioned country kitchens where families can eat is still important to some New Englanders.

How much families keep of their cultural heritage and how much they adapt to fit the pattern of day-to-day living varies with individual families. Traditional eating patterns may be observed for special occasions, while only remnants of traditions may be used from day to day in a busy home. It depends, in part, on what each family considers important— what their values are, and what compromises are necessary to fit their current life-style in the home.

Analyzing the situation may help:

How often does the family have an opportunity to communicate and interact together?

Can mealtime set the stage for this?

How many meals each day do family members eat at home?

How many meals a day do they eat together?

How much time do family members have for mealtime? Is it a leisurely time or a quick activity?

Are mealtimes structured or do they "happen," when everyone decides it's time to eat?

How flexible is the family about how to eat and where to eat?

What is the family attitude about food and eating? Is mealtime a pleasant interlude? Is it formal or informal? Is food a source of energy to be consumed quickly?

When all family members cannot eat some meals together, an area for informal meals for one or two might
be planned in the food preparation area. Emily Malino
has taken this window wall in a small kitchen and extended its apparent space with vertical blinds to frame
the view and control the light. A narrow shelf hugging
the sill becomes a counter to hold plants, creating a
pleasant area for a quick meal. A white Formica covered
rolling cart server doubles as a table for eating.
(Courtesy Window Shade Manufacturers Association)

Is eating together important?

Do some family members eat alone at different times? Why?

Are some meals considered more important
than others? Which ones? Why?

How important is "eye" appeal at mealtime,
including table accessories as well as food?

What is the family pattern regarding how food
is served:

At the table?

By the head of the household?

From the food preparation area?

Where does the family prefer to eat?

Sometimes practical considerations as well
as values influence when, where, and how a
family eats.

Factors such as:

Whether or not there is a separate dining area
in the home.

The size of the space used.

What facilities there are for food preparation,
for storage of dishes, and other accessories
for the table, and how close they are to the
area for eating.

Who is responsible for meals and meal preparation; how much time is available for
planning and preparing.

Whether or not the homemaker works.

How often there are guests for meals, and
whether they are expected or impromptu.

The ages of family members.

The work hours of some family members, and
the activity hours of others.

The responsibilities that individual family
members have outside the home, at work
or in activities.

The flexibility of space in the home for alternate eating plans as the occasion demands.

These three factors — cultural heritage,
family values, and their practical application

Lack of space need not always limit how one eats or entertains at meals. With a little creativity, an area such as a hall can be transformed into a dining area temporarily.

Two slim Parsons tables that act as hall consoles during the day fit together into a square for a dining table. The dining chairs are easy-to-store white canvas captains' chairs.

(1970 BURLINGTON HOUSE AWARD, "Efficiency Apartment for a Couple")

to the current situation—will influence how and where family members will eat in the home.

Perhaps, however, the human needs, besides the need for food, should also be considered in planning a place to eat.

Although there is evidence that many families caught up in numerous individual activities do not eat together at all, there's something to be said for families making an effort to try to have meals together as often as possible. For one thing, it does foster the need for security and belonging. If communication among family members is good, mealtime can also be the time for each member to feel important as he participates in conversations or tells about his activities of the day.

Sharing real responsibility for planning and preparing the family meal may help to meet the need for recognition and belonging.

One of the most important functions that a family meal may do is to provide the setting for family decision making. Teen-age boys, especially, according to research, spend less time at home than their sisters because they feel that they have little or no voice in family activities and decisions.* Being included in important discussions at meal time could help.

Setting the Stage for Family Meals. Meaningful family mealtimes don't just happen. They take careful planning and attention to the "nitty gritty" details as well as overall organization.

For example:
A round table is more conducive to conversation.

* Evelyn M. Duvall, "Research Finds," *Marriage and Family Living*, February 1969, p. 49.

Young children should be seated next to an adult or older sibling so that they can be helped, if needed, in eating.
Children who might tend to disrupt each other at mealtime should not be seated next to each other.
The height of a child's chair should enable him to reach the table easily.
Table talk should avoid controversial topics that will create heated arguments, since food is enjoyed more and is of more benefit when those eating are relaxed.
An occasional meal might be planned to highlight the family's cultural heritage or introduce family members to the foods and ways of people different from themselves.
Meals should be organized to facilitate ease in serving. This will vary with each family.
It could mean:
The cooking and serving of foods at the table, with all ingredients and implements organized in a given area, such as a rolling cart, or a small table next to the dining table. This requires thoughtful advance organization.
The use of cooking dishes that are attractive and practical enough to also use for serving.
The serving of the meal from the food preparation area, perhaps with each member carrying his own plate to the table.
The use of a counter as a serving table.

The alternatives are many and the mode might be varied as the family situation dictates.
An attractive table is important, too, but how it is set should be relevant to the times and to the family situation. There are many "hang-ups" about table settings that date back to other times and other needs. Finger

152

The actual place where a meal is eaten is important, too. Mention has already been made of the role of variety in providing stimulation. However, there's something to be said, too, for selecting one area in the home if it naturally provides the setting for a relaxing meal. This dining area in a houseboat with an ever constant yet changing view of the water and passing boats provides a beautiful setting for such a meal. Any interesting view from a window can serve this same purpose.
(1971 BURLINGTON HOUSE AWARD WINNER, "Man's Houseboat in Seattle")

Paintings by family members give a very personal feeling to this area for eating. They provide a setting to which individuals and family can relate. There's a touch of the old, too, in the serving buffet which was made from some old oak panelling rescued from an old bank building. Furnishings and accessories with a past contribute a feeling of stability when used in the home.
(1970 BURLINGTON HOUSE AWARD, "Young Family on the West Coast")

bowls, for example, date back to "prefork" banquets when guests ate with their fingers. It was necessary for two servants to pass among the guests—one with a bowl of water, one with a towel. In less formal situations, fingers were cleaned with bread.

In Medieval times it was the custom for the host or hostess to be served first and to taste the food first to assure guests that they were not going to be poisoned. Thus, our custom today of the hostess' eating first at a meal.

Napkins date back to the ancient Romans and Greeks. Sometimes tablecloths had long ends that also served as napkins.

And today's rounded dinner knife can be attributed to Cardinal Richlieu who ordered that the ends of knives be rounded to counter-act pointed knives being used as weapons at the dinner table.

Whether a table setting is formal with linens, silver, candlelight, and flowers, or informal with plastic place mats, paper napkins, break-resistant dishes, and stainless steel will depend on what's relevant to the family situation. The emphasis should be function.

A touch of beauty at mealtime, however, is important. It may be a touch of whimsey, a potted plant, or an interesting combination of foods on a platter.

Color coordination is also important. Attention to details helps to create the background for a meal. It does not cost more money to plan coordinated table accessories—just more time and thought. In fact, the responsibility for creating an attractive table, set to be functional for each particular meal, could very well be a

responsibility for one family member to assume. Souvenirs from family trips might serve as decorations. Or, interesting old family treasures could be used to hold bread, butter, other foods.

Arrangement of Furnishings for Eating. There is no one ideal place for eating in the home. Traditionally, it has been the dining room or the kitchen. In some homes, the living room has included a dining area. But there's no reason why eating has to take place in these areas. Practical considerations may ultimately be the determining factor.

For example:

Proximity to the source of the food-preparation area is important so that food will not become cold before it reaches the table. This source could be a portable cart equipped with food preparation facilities as easily as the kitchen.

If food is to be cooked and served at or near the table in electrical appliances, electrical outlets should be conveniently located and wiring should not cross a traffic path.

It helps to have storage for dishes and flatwear near where food will be served and not too far from where dishes are washed.

If a meal is to be eaten from a tray in an area not too near where food is prepared, consideration must be given to the traffic pattern along which the tray with food will be carried.

Lighting Needs. Lighting can influence the atmosphere or "mood" of an area for eating. A brightly lighted area with a maximum of visual contrast will encourage an eat-and-run attitude. On the other hand, an area that invites a leisurely meal will have a lower level of lighting, with some shadows on the ceiling. If the table has light, but the area surrounding it is dark (such as candlelight), people will speak in lowered voices and will eat moderate amounts of food. The same source of light on the table, but with more general illumination in the room, will encourage lively conversation and hearty appetites. A direct source of light, either on the table or providing light down on it is desirable. Additional wall lighting may also be used.

The atmosphere created for eating is a very personal decision, depending on the relative importance of this activity in the home. If the area for eating is also used for other activities, lighting needs will depend on the tasks carried on there and will need to be considered in making plans.

The number of lumens recommended per square foot for this area is 45.

Cornice lighting, such as that used at the window area in this room can provide atmosphere lighting as well as produce a dramatic effect as it directs light downward over an area. When fabric is on the surface being lighted, its texture will be emphasized.

When a wall has less than 12 inches of space between the top of the windows and the ceiling, a cornice for lighting will give an illusion of greater ceiling height.

Socialization Role of Eating. Sometimes the serving and eating of food or "breaking bread" with friends and acquaintances is an important function of a place to eat in the home, too. In many family homes, the formal dining room seems to be saved for this, along with the best dishes and silver. Perhaps this is

because the china and silver which seem a must to every bride really require more care than is anticipated, and a more practical approach seems advisable for the daily family situation.

Since home is considered an extension of self, the formal area for dining may be perpetuated as part of the "front stage" area of the home, and the formal accessories that are traditionally associated with it may be kept for "best" in order to make the impression desired.

This raises some interesting questions:
Is this type of "front stage" entertaining honest?
Does it tell family that they are not important enough to use the "best"?
Does it teach family members that it's OK to pretend to be something that you're not, to make an impression on others?
Does it lead family members to think that their daily eating routine is not very desirable or worthy of sharing with others?

Entertainment may have different space requirements and needs. There is nothing wrong with special activities for food service for guests, since it may mark a special occasion in the family routine. But it should still reflect the life-style of the family, one that all can relate to and feel comfortable with, since there is such a close connection between environment and personality. An area for eating, whether for family or guests, should be planned to encourage interaction as well. A supportive interpersonal environment provides valuable inputs to personality development and no area in the home should be exempt from careful planning to encourage this.

157

Physical Space Requirements. There are certain requirements ideally for space to sit and to eat that cannot be ignored in planning a place for eating.

For each person seated at a table, 24 inches needs to be allowed for space for dishes, glasses, utensils, as well as for comfort in eating.

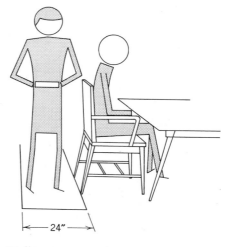

Walking past seated person

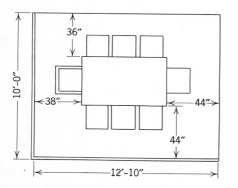

Dining areas for eight persons with free-standing table 72" × 40", one armchair, and seven armless chairs (calculated on basis of edging space on sides where there is not serving space, so that everyone can leave his place without disturbing others)

Edging past seated person

With less emphasis on formal dining, a place to eat in
the home can be almost anywhere the imagination
dreams about. Sometimes, a view by the window will
be the most desirable; another time and informal snack
in a multipurpose room may be just right. Flexibility in
planning for places to eat combined with the practicality
of furnishings and utensils which do not require extra
care is important for this kind of approach to a place
to eat.
(Courtesy Window Shade Manufacturers Association)

SOURCES OF INFORMATION

Czajkowski, Janina M. "Family Mealtime," a
    publication of The Connecticut Extension
    Services, 1964.
Duvall, Evelyn M. "Research Finds," *Marriage
    and Family Living*, February 1969, p. 49.
General Electric Company, Large Lamp Divi-
    sion, Nela Park, Cleveland, Ohio.
McCullough, K. P., Smith, R. H., Wood, A. L.,
    Woolrich, A., "Space Standards for House-
    hold Activities," *Bulletin 686*, University
    of Illinois Agricultural Experiment Station.
"Pennsylvania Dutch Foods and Traditions," a
    publication of the Cooperative Extension
    Service, College of Agriculture, The Uni-
    versity of Connecticut, Storrs, Connecticut.
"Swedish Foods and Traditions," a publication
    of the Cooperative Extension Service, Col-
    lege of Agriculture, The University of Con-
    necticut, Storrs, Connecticut.
Watts, Joanne, *The Woman's Guide to the
    Orient*, published by Japan Air Lines.

Area for Rest

Sleep is a basic biological need. Why it is needed and what role it plays in the physical and psychological needs of the human being is the unknown that is being investigated in research by psychologists and other scientists. Of especial concern is the nature, function, and meaning of mental activity during sleep, since man spends approximately one-third of his life in bed.

Sleep has been described as a period of relatively low responsiveness to sensory stimulation and of relatively little goal-directed motor activity. Regular nightly sleep is important, although the number of hours of sleep needed has not been scientifically determined. The generally held belief that eight hours of sleep are needed is not based on fact, but some attribute it to Maimonedes who centuries ago decreed "the day and night is 24 hours. It is enough for a man to sleep one third of them." *

Recent research on sleep would indicate that quality of sleep is very important. During sleep there is a progression of repeated cycles representing different phases of brain and body activity. Human beings descend level by level to deeper sleep, and with this decent comes progressively a removal from reality. There are definite stages of sleep which have been researched in laboratories.

The first is the threshold of sleep, where one is drifting off to sleep. Then comes Stage I, which to the individual may seem like drifting with idle thoughts. One may be enjoying a floating sensation — muscles are relaxing, heart rate is slowing down. In this stage, a person can be easily awakened — in fact he may not even think he was asleep. If he is not

* Gay Gaer Luce and Julius Segal, *Sleep*, Coward-McCann, Inc., New York, 1966.

disturbed, he will descend to State II. In this stage, a person may still think he hasn't been asleep, even though he could have been sleeping soundly for ten minutes.

During Stage III, the muscles are very relaxed, breathing is even, the heart rate slows, and body temperature is declining. The blood pressure also drops.

From here, the sleeper enters Stage IV which is known as delta sleep. Here, one is almost immobile, and if anyone were to try to awaken him, it would take a few seconds for the individual mind to come to the surface. If one is a sleep walker, this is the stage during which this takes place. During the first half of the night, a large portion of sleep time is spent in this Stage IV. It is a deep sleep and is sometimes called the sleep of the weary. Researchers have found that if an individual did not enter this stage of sleep for several nights that he would later compensate for it.

After descending to Stage IV, the mind gradually drifts up through Stages III, II, to I—and all this during the first 90 minutes of sleep.

But now, the individual is not back where he started, but rather in a dream period which researchers can identify by rapid eye movements in sleep—scientifically this is known as REMS. Research shows that brain wave patterns during this period resemble those of waking. Some even say that this Stage I REM is not a sleep period at all, but rather, a unique state of consciousness.

Throughout sleep, until the last hour before waking, heart rate and blood pressure continue to fall, except during the REMS periods, when there are wild fluctuations in these even though the body is quiet and the muscles are relaxed.

During the night, for the normal adult, the cycle of sleep stages is repeated 4–5 times, and each time the dream stage is longer. There are indications that all of these stages of sleep are needed by the human body.

Not all people sleep alike and not all need the same amount of sleep. Each person has his own inner timing that seems to regulate his bodily needs, day and night. Circumstances influence this, too, although they may not always be recognized.

Have you noticed that:
You sleep longer when you are deeply depressed about something?
That it's harder to wake up in the morning when you know that it's going to be an unpleasant or tense day?

All people do not approach sleep in the same way, either, although Freud states that anxiety toward sleep is universal. Some people fear sleep because they don't want to give up control over themselves. Children can think of all kinds of additional projects at bedtime to delay going to sleep. Psychiatrists describe the reluctance of children to be left alone at bedtime as a basic "separation anxiety."

Regardless of the anxieties, individuals eventually succumb because without sleep there is a loss of efficiency in mental and physical function; irritability develops, and one may find it difficult to adapt to his environment.

One of the concerns, then, in planning an area for rest is that of planning an environment that will be conducive to sleep. Although individual rest patterns vary, certain factors have been found to be basic:

Physical Comfort. The bed itself must be

suitable to the individual in degree of firmness and in size (width and length); the bed linens should be comfortable, too.

Appearance. The overall appearance of the area as well as the individual furnishings should be pleasing to the eye of the person for whom the area is planned.

Environmental Control. Facilities for controlling light, heat, and noise should be available.

When environmental stimuli are reduced to a low monotonous level, sleep is encouraged. Interestingly, scientists have found that it is possible during sleep to discriminate between meaningful stimuli. A mother, for example, may hear a baby's cry and not hear traffic noises.

Light control is especially important. Not only does it help to "set the stage" for sleep, but the length of time one sleeps may be influenced by how dark the area is in the morning.

Each individual, starting in early childhood, develops his own ritual for preparation for sleep. Some must eat a snack, listen to music, or watch the news on TV; others walk the dog, lock all the doors, or turn off all the lights. Still others may have definite theories about how to sleep. Benjamin Franklin, for example, believed cool skin was essential to relaxed sleep, so he had two beds in his room. When the first bed got warm, he left it and got into the second bed.

If individual rituals and beliefs contribute to sleep, then it's important to recognize them as such and to plan the area for rest according to individual needs.

Nowhere in the research on sleep does there seem to be any mention that a room of one's own is essential for sleep. Yet, our society which is an industrial one, puts great emphasis on individuality, and a room of one's own has become one of the symbols of this. According to anthropologists, this room of one's own is at the end of a long lonely trip to individualism, from the basinette to the play pen, to the high chair, to one's own bed, and ultimately to one's bedroom. They maintain that this actually teaches separateness, aloneness, and apartness.

Other cultures do not put the same value on a private room. The Eskimo family, still today, lives in one to two rooms with several generations. Togetherness is more important than privacy and, actually, when this support is taken away, for example, when a youngster goes away to school or work, sometimes the individual cannot "take it" and returns home, or looks for a substitute family.

In Amish homes, large bedrooms have three and four beds in them with no separate bedrooms for each child. Often, the three youngest children sleep in the bedroom with their parents. And incidentally, there is no space taken up by closets—the clothes are hung on hooks around the side of the room.

The Japanese have no bedrooms as such. Mats are spread out on the floor, and then rolled up and stored in a closet during the day.

Studies do indicate that an area for sleeping should look the part, and the bed should be an important functional piece of furniture.

The bed, in history, has had an interesting evolution. Early peoples spent more money on their construction and decoration than on any other piece of furniture.

The Egyptians, Babylonians, Assyrians, Persians, Greeks, and Etruscans all had beds of splendor, and when the Romans came along with their emphasis on material magnificence, they created beds enriched with bronze and even solid silver.

In the 15th century, the size of the bed became important, reaching to 7 or 8 feet by 6 or 7 feet, and the "best bed" was considered an important family possession. It was used as a couch for receptions during the day, and when the curtains were drawn, they completely surrounded the bed for privacy and protection from the cold at night.

The 17th century was a period of even more magnificent beds. Every part was covered with rich fabric that was very costly and the four corners of the tester had plumes or feathers mounted on them. These beds often cost more than the rest of the furniture in the house and were considered one outward sign of wealth. Even in the early days of New England, in the Plymouth Colony, the most valued piece of furniture was the bed.

It was not until the middle of the 19th century when improved heating and ventilation made bed curtains unnecessary, that the "great bed" began to be replaced by a simpler one.

In these earlier days, the bed was an important piece of furniture in the most important room in the house. Today, it is one of the functional pieces of furniture in the area for rest.

Although sleep is an important human need, an area for rest can also provide for other kinds of rest, such as emotional refreshment, a replenishment of the spirit. It can create an environment to balance human needs and foster emotional growth.

Individual concepts of the importance of this area vary. For some, it's a sanctum sanctorum, a private world to retreat to from the activities of family and work, a place to screen one from outside forces; it may be an area to call one's own, to satisfy the need for territoriality, a haven to find refuge for thinking, listening, studying, and dreaming—a place to express one's personality. In many homes, this area is traditionally a bedroom. Sometimes it's a room of one's own; sometimes it's shared with brothers, sisters, or husband and wife.

For those with too much family and too little space, the need for rest and the other needs for privacy and territoriality may need to be met in some other way.

Creating a Meaningful Environment. A bedroom, perhaps more than any other area in the home, can provide an opportunity for self-expression and an opportunity to develop self-confidence. Regardless of age, decisions concerning the selection of furnishings can be exercised, ranging from a limited choice within a preselected group of colors for furnishings in a young child's room, to a total freedom to furnish the entire room for a teen-ager.

Because an area for rest is usually "back stage" for a family home, it can have the flexibility to change as individuals grow and develop so that it always remains a meaningful environment within which individual growth is encouraged, without the concern for the impression of others that the "front-stage" areas have.

Even with more than one sharing an area, there can be opportunities for self-expression as well as lessons in socializing, since in a shared-room situation there is an added dimension—that of learning to consider more than one point of view in furnishing a room. This can well be an experience in itself that will pay dividends in later years when a family home is being furnished.

164

In their remodeled barn, Mr. & Mrs. T. Donahue have two large sleeping quarters for their children and their guests,—a boys' dormitory and a girls' dormitory. These are no-nonsense areas for sleep, with no sensory stimuli for distraction. The old bicycle mounted on the wall is part of their collection of antiques—one of their roots with the past.
(Courtesy Mr. & Mrs. Theodore Donahue, Photography by Howard Graff)

Since sleeplessness interfers with the body's energy metabolism, it's important to plan an area for rest carefully to set the stage for relaxation and sleep according to needs of the individual. If T.V. and hi-fi are part of the nightly ritual before sleep, space should be planned for them. In this small room, a minimal amount of space has been taken to create a wall-to-wall storage unit. The window shades serve as room darkeners for light control (they can also control noise to a degree). There's even space to put a tray holding a bed-time snack. Still another factor incorporated for relaxation is the adjustable beds that can be electrically controlled for reclining as well as lying flat. (Courtesy Window Shade Manufacturers Association)

To express individuality, sometimes just a corner to call one's own is enough. In a home, such as the one shown here. Without enough space for a separate area for rest, this has been very effectively done with Indian art, reflecting personal interests on the wall area around the bed. It can only be enjoyed when the doors are opened and the bed comes out of the closet, but it is still there, and accessible when needed.
(1970 BURLINGTON HOUSE AWARD, "Efficiency Apartment")

Analysis of Activities and Needs for Furnishings

Creating an environment for rest ultimately involves planning the use of available space to suit an individual need. Besides the generic needs for rest, an analysis of individual needs to be satisfied and activities to be carried out in the area is a necessary step. Then, an appraisal of the furnishings needed to carry out these activities must be made to determine if there is adequate space and how it will be arranged.

In carrying out this analysis, these questions should be considered:

Is the rest area part of another functional area, or is it a room or section of the home planned especially for this?

How much space is available?

What activities must be confined to this room, and which might be carried on in some other area in the home?

What are the furnishings needed to carry out each activity?

How much space will each activity require?

Will the storage of clothing and will dressing be functionally a part of the area? If so, what furnishings are needed? What kind of storage is desired? What kind of space is available?

If the area is a room for one:

Is there other space available in the home, or must all activities of personal interest be centered in this room?

If all activities of personal interest are centered in this area, will this be encouraging aloneness? What alternate plans can be made to provide this individual with opportunities for involvement with other family members?

Is this area to be a "private world," or will it serve the traditional role of bedroom?

Is this to be the center for personal creative activities? If so, what furnishings are needed and what type of space arrangement is required for these activities?

How much space is needed for clothing storage and dressing needs?

If the area is to be shared:

How many must share this area and what is their relationship?

How much space is available? Is it flexible?

Will it be possible to provide for some privacy for each individual sharing the room?

Will they be able to communicate and still have a private area to retreat to if they wish to?

What activities will each want to carry on in the room? What furnishings will be needed to carry them out?

Which will be shared activities?

Which might be carried on in some other area in the home?

Are the individuals who share this room compatible, or is there a need to provide for individual space divisions?

Is there opportunity for each to pursue individual creative expressions? Is there a way to combine their likes into a coordinated whole?

Is there an age difference that will influence types of activities and furnishings planned for the area?

How much space is needed for the storage of clothing and for dressing?

If the area for rest is part of another area in the home:

What other activities are carried on in the area?

Will any of them interfere with the person resting?

Is there a way to arrange the area to shield the area for rest, if the room is to be used for more than one activity at a time?

Is there a way to reduce stimuli to a low level? Is there a way to darken the room, to block out noises?

Needs for Dress. Traditionally, if the area for rest is separate from other areas, the functions of dress and storage of clothing are also a part of it. Assuming that they are, an analysis of the steps in dressing and the needs for storage of clothing will include these questions:

How much time is needed to get dressed in the morning?

If there is more than one sharing the room, will one be asleep while the other is dressing? If so, will this influence the amount of light that can be used?

Does the decision about what to wear the next day need to be made before going to bed? If the decision is made the night before, are the clothes laid out then, or are they removed from storage just before dressing?

If they are laid out the night before, how much space is needed and what kind? How many flat surfaces? How many hooks for hangers?

What about undressing? Where do soiled clothes get placed when they are removed? Is there a way to sort them in separate storage units for ease in organizing the laundry?

Is there a need for a place to empty pockets before undressing?

Where are clothes that are worn for sleeping stored? How do they need to be stored? Are they hung? Are they folded?

Is clothing to wear to bed within easy reach of the area where daytime clothing is removed?

What about organized storage for shoes, hats, and accessories so that they can be easily identified when needed?

How much flat storage for clothing is needed? How many things need to be hung?

Is there a need for a place to sit for dressing?

Is grooming part of the dressing ritual? Is it desirable to do it in the dressing area? If so, how much space is needed for grooming needs? If not enough space is available, where else can it be done? Is grooming carried out standing up or sitting down?

For storage of clothing. Basically, the functions of storage for clothing are to protect it from dust, to keep it free from wrinkling, and to help it maintain its shape between uses. Clothes also need ventilation where stored.

Certain basic measurements are desirable and should be considered when clothing storage is being planned.

- The minimum depth of closet — 24 inches
- The minimum width of closet per person (this will vary with the individual and the amount of clothing) — 48 inches
- The depth of shelves — 12 inches
- The average rod space per garment
  - women's — 2 inches
  - men's — $2\frac{1}{2}$ inches
- The height of rod from floor for street-length clothes — 63 inches
- The distance between rod and shelf above it — $2\frac{1}{2}$ inches
- The distance between closet hooks — 7 inches

Here, a suggestion for two private halves of a closet starts with a fabric panel divider held taut by two curtain rods. The top rod can be suspended from the bottom of the shelf at the midway point of the closet, and the bottom rod fastened to the floor. Then, each of the principles of storage can be applied individually to arrange each half according to personal needs.

A step shelf divides the top shelf into two. See-through boxes reveal contents for easy identification. A long box on top shelf may store an evening dress in between uses. Heavy equipment, such as a typewriter sits on the floor, as does a suitcase which might double as a storage unit between uses.
(Courtesy J.C. Penney Company, Inc.)

Arrangement of Furnishings

If this area is to satisfy many human needs, there may be more than one center of activity, all of equal importance.

Bed Area. Certain needs are generic, regardless of where the area for rest is located, or how much space is available.

A bed of some kind, with suitable bed linens, and a cover for warmth. Of course, it must fit the space available.

A light source that can be easily reached from the bed. To be functional, it should be easy to turn off from a lying position in bed, and be sturdy enough so that it will not break if accidentally knocked over.

Not absolutely basic, but certainly helpful:

A time source within range of the eye. Ideally, the dial figures should be discernible in the dark, and some kind of alarm may be desirable. It helps, too, if it is a quiet clock.

A flat surface (table, box, and the like) next to the bed, possibly to hold a light source and a clock, as well as being a place to put reading matter, glasses, or even snacks. It should be of a height that can be easily reached by the person lying in bed.

A rug on which to step when getting out of bed.

A telephone next to the bed so that it will be convenient in case of emergencies.

A TV that can be seen from the bed and, a desirable luxury, a control for the TV next to the bed.

Lighting Needs

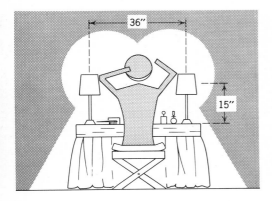

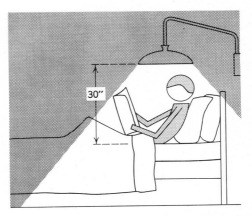

Grooming. Whether shaving or applying makeup, this visual task is a very critical one. Recommended footcandles are: 50

The light source at the mirror should direct light toward the person and *not* the mirror. It helps to have light from three directions—above and the two sides.

The center of the shades should be at cheek height of the person using the grooming area, so a basic decision about whether grooming will be done sitting or standing needs to be made before lamps are selected.

Lamp shades should be highly translucent and there should be a distance of 2″ from the top of the bulb to the top of the shade to prevent seeing the bulb when standing.

Surrounding walls should have a reflectance of at least 50 percent, including the surface below the mirror.

The light sources should be inside the 60° visual cone.

Reading in Bed. The light source should be placed so that it does not create shadows on the materials being read. Also, of course, it should not interfere with the comfort of the person reading.

If a table lamp is used, the center of the base should be in line with the shoulder. When the person is in a semi-reclining position, the lower edge of the shade should be at eye level, and the lamp should be 22″ to the left or right of the center of the book or paper being read.

Ideal lamp shade dimensions are a 15–17″ bottom, an 8–15″ top, and a depth of 10–14″.

General illumination may also be provided by valence lighting as well as other light sources.

If grooming needs are taken care of in the bathroom, the same lighting guidelines will apply. Note mirror with light directed toward the person.
(Courtesy General Electric Company, Large Lamp Department)

Adequate lighting at bedside can be individually controlled here and provides privacy from unwanted light if desired. The general illumination is additional when more light is needed.
(Courtesy General Electric, Large Lamp Division)

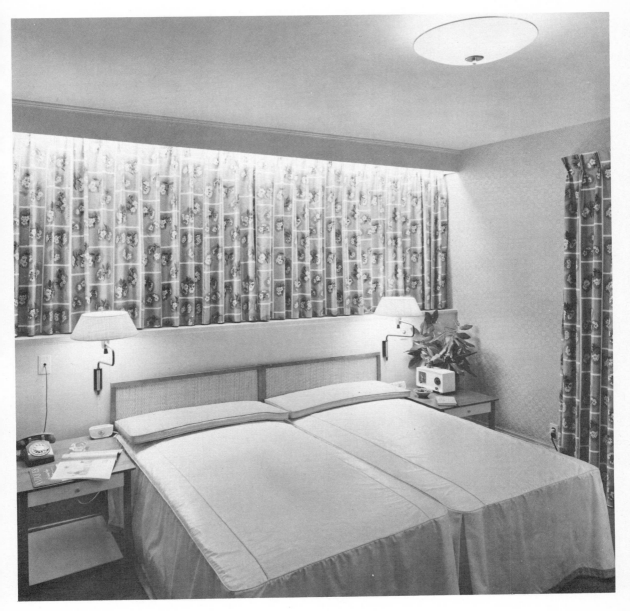

Physical Space Needs. Space considerations in this area for cleaning and making the
bed include:

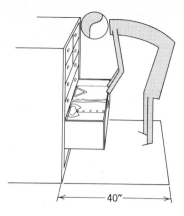

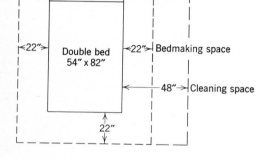

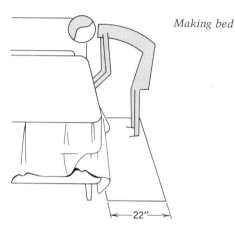

Making bed

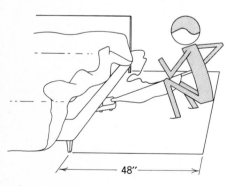

Cleaning under bed

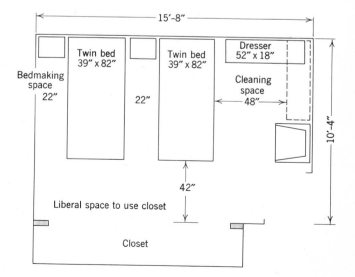

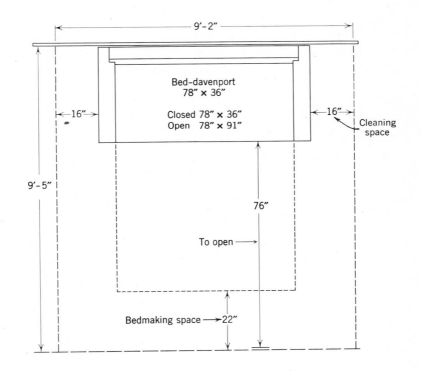

9′-2″

Bed-davenport
78″ × 36″

Closed 78″ × 36″
Open 78″ × 91″

16″

16″

Cleaning space

9′-5″

76″

To open →

Bedmaking space → 22″

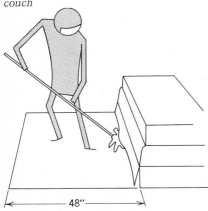

Cleaning under bed-davenport or studio couch

48″

Cleaning ends of bed-davenport

16″

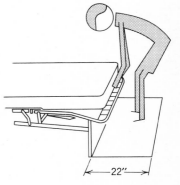

Opening or making bed-davenport

22″

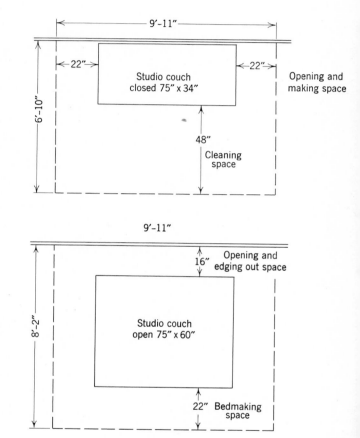

—16"—

—22"—

9'-11"

22" · Studio couch closed 75" x 34" · 22" · Opening and making space

6'-10"

48"

Cleaning space

9'-11"

16" · Opening and edging out space

8'-2" · Studio couch open 75" x 60"

22" · Bedmaking space

In this room, designed by Emily Malino, the furnishings have been arranged to meet basic needs: The light source is within easy reach, there is a flat surface next to the bed on which to place reading matter and snacks, and the telephone is convenient if needed. (Courtesy Window Shade Manufacturers Association)

Two sisters who may have different interests and different color preferences can find a way to compromise. Here, a print using the favorite colors of each is used for the curtain and dust ruffles. Each bedspread, however, picks up the color from the print that is the individual favorite.
A small room such as this without much space that must be shared by two would function best for contact people. There's respect for territoriality in the individualized beds, but most activities in the rest of the room would need to be shared.
(Courtesy J.C. Penney Company, Inc.)

Psychological Space Must Be Considered

As in other areas in the home, psychological space needs are an important consideration in planning an area for rest, whether it is a room for one, or an area shared with others. Perhaps here, more than anywhere else in the home, every individual needs to understand his or her own space needs, to know what the personal space bubble will tolerate, and how often privacy will be needed.

In planning for these needs, some of the questions which should be considered are:

What type of environment best suits the individual needs—a quiet shield from the outside world, including the rest of the family, or lively space?

Is this the only place in the home for privacy for the individuals involved?

Are the individuals contact or noncontact personalities? If the room is shared, are both types involved? If so, how can the needs of each be met?

If shared by more than one, will each individual have an area to call his own?

If the area is small, can it be arranged to give an illusion of space?

Here, an area shared by two, is carefully planned for separate but equal space for rest and study by each. It could function equally well for non-contact people whose areas need to be clearly defined, as well as for contact personalities who would use the entire room as one area.
(Courtesy J.C. Penney Company, Inc.)

Certainly, the tranquility of this child's room would encourage relaxation and help provide a suitable background for stage I of sleep. The bed is Finnish, made of painted white birch. A Le Corbusier crucifix from La Tourette adorns the white wall under the eaves. The bed has its own trundle underneath, for an overnight guest and the top bar of the bed can be removed when a child is old enough not to fall out. Special shelves provide a place to store toys.
(1970 BURLINGTON HOUSE AWARD WINNER, "Young Family in Connecticut." Photo Courtesy of Glamour, © 1970 Conde Nast Publications, Inc.)

An area for rest for some may literally be their private world, the one room they have for self-expression, for relaxation and for entertainment. Here a narrow space with imagination and creativity has been turned into an attractive sitting-bedroom. The mocha walls and a brown and black striped sofa bed keep the room unified in color. A wall of window shades conceals the one window and makes the room appear wider. (Courtesy Window Shade Manufacturers Association)

SOURCES OF INFORMATION

Foulkes, David, *The Psychology of Sleep,*
    Charles Scribner's Sons, New York, 1966.
Luce, Gay Gaer, and Segal, Julius, *Sleep,*
    Coward-McCann, Inc., New York, 1966.
McCullough, K. P., Smith, R. H., Wood, A. L.,
    Woolrich, A., "Space Standards for House-
    hold Activities," *Bulletin 686,* University
    of Illinois Agricultural Experiment Station.
The Bed, A catalog from an exhibit at the
    Museum of Contemporary Crafts, 29 West
    53rd Street, New York, N.Y., 1966.

Storage

Storage in the home is a challenge to every family member, since the organization of one's tools and supplies for activities or possessions, whether they are utensils for food preparation, hobbies, toys, or clothes, is basic to an orderly life.

As in planning the furnishings for each area, storage must be carefully planned, too.

Each activity should be analyzed in relation to the following:

The kinds of equipment or supplies needed that must be stored.

Where an activity will be carried on; this may be very personal and not related to traditional concepts.

How often stored equipment or articles will be used. (Everyday? Once a week? Seasonally?)

The dimensions of equipment or articles that need to be stored.

The type of storage suitable. (Shelves? Drawers? Closets? Dual purpose furniture?)

The personal habits and preferences of individuals using equipment or supplies.

Any limiting factors in relation to the equipment or the activity. For example, some supplies for photography must be stored away from light; most leftover food must be stored, covered, in a cool place; a typewriter is heavy and needs to be stored at the point of use to avoid excessive lifting.

Expenditures of energy needed to reach for items stored. The easy reach area, with elbows bent, requires the least expenditure of energy; maximum reach area, with arms outstretched, requires more energy. Storage beyond these reach areas will require considerable energy to reach and should be reserved for those items not used frequently.

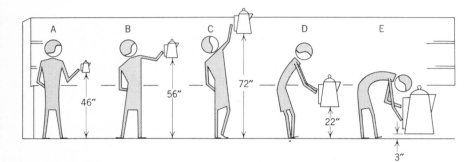

Easy
Reach
Area

Varying amounts of energy are needed to reach different distances. Based on the reach of a woman 5 feet 3 inches tall, the following holds true:

reaching up to 46 inches from the floor takes the least energy.

reaching to 56 inches requires twice as much energy.

bending to reach 22 inches above the floor requires more than 4½ times as much energy.

bending to reach 3 inches above the floor requires more than 11 times as much energy.

Once storage needs for activities are carefully analyzed, they become individual storage problems to be solved.

There are nine basic principles for storage that can be applied to any storage problem in the home.

They are:
1. Items should be stored where they will be used first.
2. All items used together should be stored together.
3. Stored items should be easy to locate at a glance.
4. Like articles should be stored or grouped together.
5. All items used regularly should be stored within an area of easy reach.
6. All items should be easy to grasp at the point of storage.
7. All items should be easily removed without removing other items first.
8. Heavy equipment should be stored at or near floor level.
9. All space should be utilized for utmost efficiency.

Sometimes a combination of principles will apply in working out convenient storage. The important point is to learn to think through the problem and to understand how to apply the principles. Individually applied, the principles can be interpreted in a number of ways.

1. Store Items Where They Will Be Used First. With a little preliminary thought, it's easy enough to plan where to store items in relation to use.

If tasks and working patterns are analyzed, storage can be planned to meet the step-by-step needs of each job. For example, in meal preparation if water is used, some pans should be stored near the source of water. Others may be stored near the range. Spoons for stirring will probably be most used at the range, so storage for them should be planned to be within easy reach.

Soaps and cleaning supplies for dishes are logically stored near the sink for use in dishwashing. Spices, which are usually used at point of cooking, belong within easy reach of the range.

Sometimes, some tools may be necessary for activities carried on in more than one area. For example, measuring cups and spoons might be needed at the sink for measuring liquids into pans, and at the mixing area for measuring ingredients for baking. In this case, two sets of tools might be more efficient, with each placed at point of use.

Or, it may be efficient to have duplicates of things such as aspirins, bandages, and pencils in places where they might be logically needed or handy.

The same kind of thinking can be applied to the storage of clothing.

For example, is there a particular area where each individual dresses? Are outer garments and undergarments all within close proximity, so that they don't have to be gathered from different areas and brought to one spot?

What about soiled clothing? Where will it be stored? A receptacle of some kind, whether a box, a hamper, or a basket, placed at the point where clothing is removed, will save steps. More than one receptacle, placed at the same point, can provide the means for sorting the laundry as it is removed—one can be for delicate washables, another for sturdy ones. A third might possibly be used for the items, for instance, men's shirts or sheets, that will be sent to the commercial laundry.

Storage of accessories such as jewelry and cosmetics should be planned for point of use, too. In fact, both usually require the use of a mirror, so why not store them near one, not far from the dressing area?

An easily overlooked group of necessities, and one that can cause real frustration if misplaced, is family keys, especially car keys. Carefully planned storage, at the point where one leaves the house to go to the car, might be considered the point of use.

187

Here is a creative approach to storing items where they will be used first. This troth-like shelf built under the range files a good supply of pans and covers. (Reprinted by special permission from *LADIES HOME JOURNAL*, copyright Downe Publishing Company, photograph by Ernst Readle)

In the food preparation area to the right, a coffee percolator and some pans are stored near where they will be used first—at the sink. (Courtesy of Kitchens by Coppes-Napanee, Nappanee, Indiana)

189

2. All Items Used Together Should Be Stored Together. When thinking through the steps to carry out an activity, it is also logical to think through all the items needed to carry it out. If they are itemized, storage space can be planned so that all the tools or items used together can be stored together. This saves time and energy.

Some applications might be:

Recipe books, paper, and pencil can be grouped together.

Supplies and equipment for baking could be stored in a mix center.

Paper, foil, tape, and marking pens for freezing are used together.

Rainwear — boots, umbrella, and raincoat — could be placed in a closet, ideally, near the door to go out.

Stationery, something to write with, stamps, and address book belong together, at or near a place to write.

Hobby supplies may have to be in a box on a shelf, if there's no room to keep them where they will be used. Keeping all supplies together in one unit or grouping will make it easier to locate them and will save time and energy in setting up.

These cabinets by Wood-Mode Cabinetry have been designed to apply this principle. Note how easily stored items can be identified and grasped.

3. Stored Items Should Be Easy To Locate at a Glance. See-through containers not only reveal their contents at a glance but, in the case of food, they also indicate the quantity of each item on hand, so that the need to be replenished can be recognized before the supply is exhausted.

Canned goods, stored on narrow shelves are easy to identify, and eliminate "searching" for the wanted can in the back of a deep shelf.

Perforated hardboard can provide flexible storage for shelves, hanging tools, pans, and potholders.

Contents of drawers, organized in compartments (which could be boxes) keep like items together as well as making their identification easy.

Toys placed on shelves (that are within easy reach) can be decorative as well as easy to locate.

Gardening tools hung on a wall or organized on shelves can save time, energy, and nerves. This can also be a safety factor.

Keys hung on a wall, or organized in a drawer, can be color coded with tags and corresponding hooks or drawer liners for easy identification.

This storage unit is an example of the application of principle #4 which is explained on the next page. Like items are stored together according to size and use so they can be easily seen and removed. (Courtesy of Kitchens by Coppes-Napanee, Nappanee, Indiana)

4. Like Articles Should Be Stored or Grouped Together. It stands to reason that when one wants to look for necessities, such as dishes, silverware, baking pans, socks, underwear, gloves, jewelry, and ties, it is helpful to have each group stored together so that they are easy to find. Of course, it helps still further to have the components of each group organized, too—forks together, spoons together, earrings, necklaces, and cuff links together, and so on.

Canned goods, organized in storage units according to likeness of contents are easy to locate, become a visual inventory when replacements are considered.

Supplies for home repairs, especially nails, screws, and other small pieces, that are separated by size or function and stored accordingly can save hours of time when one is needed for a job.

If creative needlework is a hobby, organized storage of different colors of yarns can contribute to ease and efficiency. Grouping yarns by colors and weights can prevent twisting and knotting and could be a decorative factor as well.

5. All Items Used Regularly Should Be Stored Within an Area of Easy Reach. The easy reach area, since it requires the least expenditure of energy, should be used for the storage of those items used regularly.

As each activity is analyzed, the items needed to carry it out can be listed, and storage then can be planned within the least energy expenditure area for the items used most frequently.

One area where this principle should be applied more frequently is the study. Much time could be saved if pencils, pencil sharpener, paper, wastebasket, and references (such as a dictionary) were all within the area of easy reach. If radio and TV are important to this area, it would be ideal to be able to turn them on or off without leaving the desk or table.

Another application is thinking through what needs to be stored next to the bed. Having the light switch within easy reach is a safety factor as well as an efficiency measure. The telephone and an alarm clock for some people are also needed within easy reach.

In all instances, storage space should be analyzed carefully to be certain that it is as functional as possible in relation to how the individual will work in carrying out an activity. Sometimes additional storage can be created to make space available within the easy reach area with devices such as perforated hardboard and open shelving.

Still applying principle #5, easy reach needs to be considered in relation to the individual.
In a child's room, this means that storage needs to be low enough so that it is within easy reach of the person using it, rather than an adult. Also, storage in a child's room needs to be flexible enough to change as the child grows.
(Courtesy West Point Pepperell)

6. All Items Should Be Easy to Grasp at Point of Storage. Deep drawers with vertical dividers hold baking dishes, racks, and lids. They are easy to find at a glance, and are easy to grasp for removal.

Tools arranged in an easy-reach area adjacent to work centers are easy to identify as well as to grasp.

Clothing can be organized, too.

Shallow storage for toys will make it easier for children to grasp individual pieces. An unpainted bookcase, used with its back parallel to the floor, could have casters put under it to roll easily under the bed. This would provide ample room to store playthings, and toys would be easy to grasp.

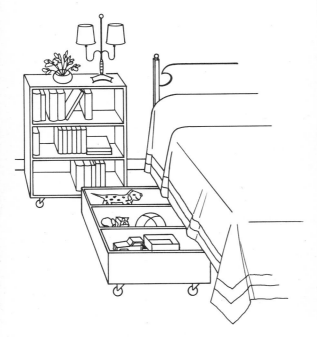

Both arrangements of drawers below have organized storage so that items are readily recognized and easily removed without removing other items first. The portable tray unit is designed by Mutschler of Nappannee Indiana, and the vertical storage is by Wood-Mode cabinetry.

7. All Items Should Be Easily Removed Without Removing Other Items First. This can prevent breakage as well as save energy.

Step shelves can be built to divide the space in cupboards where shelves are spaced far apart. They will provide the additional surfaces needed to store items and can be used to store towels, sheets, and table linens, as well as for separating dishes by sizes and functions.

Vertical storage for pots and pans can eliminate the problem of stacking pans one inside the other, so that each can be removed without removing others.

Purses might also be stored this way.

Two types of step shelves are shown here, both easy to make. Placed on closet shelves, they divide space so that possessions may be stored without being placed on top of each other.

When there are no storage facilities, they can be created. These wicker baskets are relatively inexpensive and can be put on shelves to hold all kinds of things. Knowing the contents is no different than remembering what each dresser drawer holds.

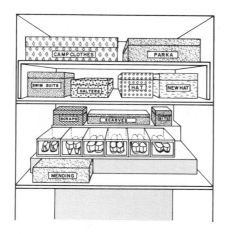

8. Heavy Equipment Should Be Stored at or Near Floor Level. Heavy appliances used infrequently can be stored in areas not within that of the easy reach. However, one needs to think through how they will be removed from the storage area, as well as how they will be put there, before storage is planned.

For example, a heavy or bulky appliance stored on a high shelf could accidentally fall on the person removing it from storage. Furthermore, its weight will be difficult to balance from a height. Heavy appliances or equipment placed near floor level will be easier to lift because the entire body can be used as leverage. It will also take less energy to place heavy equipment at a storage point near the floor than at a place above the easy-reach area.

This can be applied not only to food preparation items but to typewriters, luggage, and sports equipment.

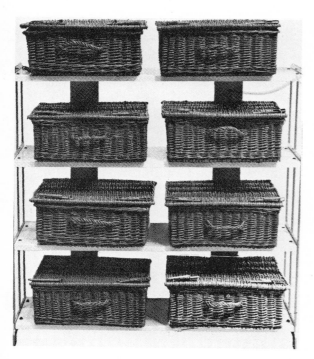

9. All Space Should Be Utilized for Utmost Efficiency. Not only does this principle apply to the efficient use of available space, as is illustrated by these blouses hung above skirts in this closet, but it can also apply to what is stored. Each item to be stored might be put to a "two-year test." If it has not been used, cleaned, or worn for 2 years, would it be better to discard it or give it away, rather than to have it take up valuable storage space?

Some Additional Generalizations about Storage

When analyzing storage needs, thought should be given to the items for each activity which might be acquired in the foreseeable future—perhaps, there will be a growing library of books, additional hobby equipment, a sewing machine, or a growing woodworking shop.

It is best to create adjustable storage facilities when possible so that they can be flexible enough to meet changing needs.

Ease of care of storage facilities must also be considered. Surfaces should be smooth, and all areas should be easy to reach for cleaning.

When space is at a premium, seasonal items may be stored out of the way of daily usage, and the principles of storage may be applied to their use only for those periods of the year when they become an important part of everyday activity. Spaces under beds and inside suitcases are ideal for this type storage.

Functional storage need not be dull. There's plenty of opportunity to be creative—to turn a storage problem into an imaginative asset, to introduce a bit of whimsey, or even a tie with the past. An old family mug, no longer practical for serving beverages, might be used to hold stirring spoons at point of use near the range; an entire wall may be converted into storage units that add color and design to an otherwise plain room; clear jars to hold food stuffs can be arranged on open shelves in the food preparation area for a practical inventory of supplies as well as a decorative asset; old furniture may be resurrected from attics and basements to fulfill new roles.

A basic understanding of the elements of design can be helpful in planning storage which is both functional and decorative.

A large bathroom in an old house can be utilized for considerable storage. Towels, bathing needs, as well as a grooming center could be built along one wall. (Courtesy J.C. Penney Company, Inc.)

THE
ROLE
OF
DESIGN

Understanding Design

The role of beauty in our lives cannot be measured in precise terms, but its value is as important as the air we breathe or the vitamins we consume. It provides the "nourishment for the soul" that can lift the mind from everyday tensions and problems to loftier thoughts and dreams. An advertisement of many years ago, showing a young child in a wooded glen, made a poetic statement about the importance of beauty with these words:

were you searching for tomorrow
with your tiger by your side?
    or was it in rebellion
that you slipped away to hide?
    how quickly you discarded cares
in this enchanted dell . . . when
    the beauty of the butterfly
caught you in its spell
    remember, nymph, this moment . . .
for, in beauty, there is peace
    . . . and, from today's
insistent world of tensions . . . a release
    whatever fills your future . . .
laughter, anger, joys, or sorrows . . .
    grant the world of beauty
its fair share in your tomorrow.

What is beauty anyway? History shows that every culture has produced objects that meet the accepted criteria for beauty.

Euripedes said, "Beauty is that which when seen is loved."

Isamo Noguchi, a contemporary Japanese designer, describes it as the fragility of things—the impermanence of beauty.

The final definition must by necessity be a personal one. So many of the inputs into each human mind and soul shape an individual's concept of beauty—cultural heritage, family influence, education, the neighborhood in which one lives, work, recreation, and friends. It should be a dynamic concept, one that changes as the individual grows and develops toward his own potential.

Beauty can be one of the major factors in the home to provide sensory intake and stimulation for the brain. Psychologists have found that a normal person placed in an atmosphere where there is little or no sensory stimulation will, in about 12 hours, hallucinate, become paranoid, and think in a chaotic and disorganized way. A monotonous environment can be considered a serious form of sensory deprivation.

Unfortunately, aesthetics in our society is not prized very highly in the value system. Beauty has not been included in the listings of important American values which have been made by sociologists or anthropologists.

Studies investigating values, where beauty is on the list, have consistently shown it to be held in low esteem. It somehow cannot be equated with the Puritan Ethic of work or with the values of time, energy, and money.

Actually, not much is known about man's aesthetic need. Maslow includes it in his hierarchy, although not in a clearly defined position (see p. 5). It is not below self-actualization, so it is possible to conclude that the need for self-actualization must be gratified before aesthetically oriented behaviors emerge with any degree of potency. Although he admits to knowing less about the aesthetic need than about the other basic needs, he has included it in his hierarchy on the premise that man has inherent cravings that can be satisfied only by beauty.

The self-actualizing person as described by Maslow perceives reality more efficiently than does the average man. He accepts himself, others, nature, and his environment positively, and focuses on problems outside himself more than on his own problems. He identifies deeply with human beings in general, and has a genuine desire to help the human race.

When the basic needs are gratified, according to Maslow, unmotivated behaviors emerge and other aesthetically oriented phenomena appear. The need for beauty, its components of symmetry, and its dimensions of suitability and perfection are satisfied. Taste improves, and a richer more positive emotional life ensues. The individual becomes more creative and more interested in the arts. Perception becomes more acute, more realistic, and less categorized. Preference for the familiar diminishes, and the unfamiliar and unstructured feel more comfortable.

It would seem, then, if Maslow is right, that helping individuals to satisfy their deep craving for beauty, can be an important factor in helping them to develop to their fullest potential.

Thus, the role of design in the home becomes a significant one in the human experience — almost a sensuous experience, to be enjoyed and appreciated for its contribution to an inherent need for beauty as well as for the psychological stimulation it provides.

This type of experience with beauty requires more than just a knowledge of design principles. It requires sensitivity and awareness on the part of the individuals who live in the home so that they can feel empathy and appreciation for the beauty around them. It means helping individuals to look for and plan design in the little things as well as the big — the arrangement of food on a platter, the design created by a shadow on a wall, the color of a bar of soap, daily change in growing plants, the experience of texture, as well as the selection and arrangement of furniture in a room, the selection of patterns to use together, and the flow of design from one object to another. It means encouraging individuals to learn how to enjoy beauty, to respond to it with the senses, to follow it with the eye but to feel it with the soul.

Although home cannot be the lone factor that creates this sensitivity, it can provide the setting which encourages individuals to respond to their environment, to reach out and enjoy the beauty around them.

As a base for planning this kind of humanly meaningful environment, a working knowledge of design and its elements serves as a guide to evaluate choices and to build confidence in one's decisions, rather than a set of "rules" to be used arbitrarily.

The following pages in this chapter have been planned to help individuals develop a sensitivity to design. Each of the elements has been presented as a visual experience. Brief explanations are followed by many illustrations which have been selected and spaced to involve you as an individual in deciding what appeals to you and what you think is beautiful. As you study the various elements, and begin to develop an awareness of your concept of beauty, you may change some of your original choices. This is all part of developing a sensitivity to and understanding of design and learning how you want to apply it to create a beautiful environment.

SOURCES OF INFORMATION

Anderson, Donald M., *Elements of Design,* Holt, Rinehart, and Winston, Inc., New York, 1961.

Beitler, Ethel Jane and Bill Lockhart, *Design for You,* John Wiley and Sons, New York, 1961.

Bevlin, Marjorie Elliott, *Design Through Discovery,* Holt, Rinehart, and Winston, Inc., New York, 1963.

Collier, Graham, *Form, Space, and Vision,* Prentice-Hall, Inc., Englewood Cliffs, N.J.

Montgomery, James E., "Impact of Housing Patterns on Marital Interaction," *The Family Coordinator,* July 1970.

Nygren, Maie, "Beauty in the American Value System: A case for Education in Aesthetics," a presentation at the 54th Annual Meeting of the American Home Economics Association.

Van Dommelen, David B., *Designing and Decorating Interiors,* John Wiley and Sons, New York, 1965.

Warner, Esther S., *Art: an Everyday Experience,* Harper & Row, New York, 1963.

line

Line is a versatile element. Basically, it outlines the limits of a form and defines its function. For example,

The lines of these objects can be easily identified by the eye. So, too, can the function of each.

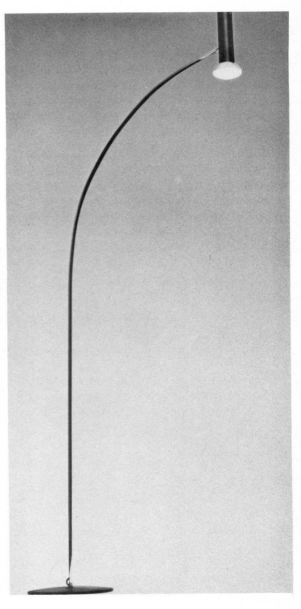

However, there's much more to it than that. Line can involve the eye and influence how one feels in a room. One can readily feel empathy with the action created by lines. For example,

The lines of this design are "active." They carry the eye up and down at sharp angles. Used as a dominant pattern in a room, it could create the feeling of fatigue for some people because the eye is continually moving. The same kind of design, however, in a small area, can create interest—an element for the eye to enjoy, at will, or to leave for a more restful surface, if desired.

(Courtesy Selig Manufacturing Company)

On the other hand, some people like a lively environment. It has been said that rock music, enjoyed by young people today is so stimulating that they need more intense colors and activity around them to keep up the momentum. For them, an active design such as this on the walls of a room can be stimulating for conversation, interaction.
(Courtesy Wallcovering Industry Bureau)

Opposite page:
(1971 BURLINGTON HOUSE AWARD WINNER "Home By The Sea" submitted by Robert Dougherty Building Products Guides)

Dwarf Dragon Tree
(Courtesy Everett Conklin).

Line can imply action in other ways, too.

Some examples of this in the home are:
A plant that is fairly dominant in an area.
   The sweep of a staircase.
A group of objects, placed in increasing or
   decreasing order of size.
A wall sculpture designed with many diagonal
   lines. This one shown below, gives a
   definite impression of flight.

(Courtesy Gump's, San Francisco)

Wood Sculpture by John and Eileen Lee
(Courtesy of the American Crafts Council, New York, New York)

Sometimes, too many lines, used in competition, can also create fatigue and frustration for the eye. For example,

Sculpture or art objects with many details, especially subtle ones, are planned for the eye to explore and enjoy as it travels from one part to another. Placed against a surface with equally detailed lines, the beauty of both becomes lost in the competition for attention that meets the eye.

This does not mean that design cannot be used with design, successfully. It can be done. But the combination must have a degree of harmony and unity, and it must also be a personal choice—one that appeals to an individual sense of design.

The room setting shown on the opposite page, and the one on the following page, both illustrate this. Each has a unifying factor. One repeats the theme of a design (following page); the other has a dominant color plan (black and white) shown on opposite page.

Sometimes, line can involve individuals emotionally—that is, it can soothe and uplift the spirit with its beauty, as illustrated by the carving below.

Joshua Tree
(Courtesy Everett Conklin)

Line can be put to work, too.

It Can Create an Illusion of Height. When line is used in a definite vertical, the eye is carried up and down, and an illusion of height is created.

When practically applied to the home, this can be translated into:

Draperies that go from the floor to the top of windows, or even the ceiling. The line created by the window treatment, as well as the vertical folds in the draperies themselves, all contribute to the illusion of height.

A vertical design on wallpaper or that is woven in fabric.

A vertical object, in an already vertical space, such as a tall clock in a narrow wall area, a curio cabinet, bookcase, or a plant.

Some examples are shown on the following pages.

Line may also be applied in the arrangement of objects such as:

Pictures placed in a vertical line

A floral arrangement

An object that already has vertical lines, used to lift the eye and sometimes the spirit

The emphasis of a vertical by placing it in contrast to its surroundings, such as a door painted in contrast to the walls.

The repetition of a vertical line to emphasize height. The lines formed by the 4 × 4 posts used to create an entrance hallway in the home shown on the opposite page are repeated in the lamp and legs of table.

A grouping of furniture and accessories together to form a vertical.

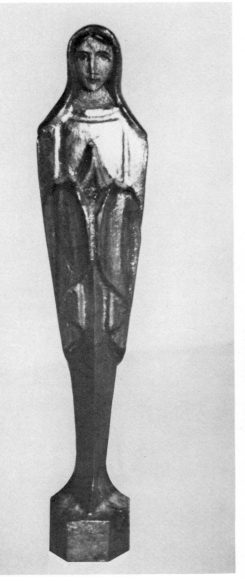

Line Can Seem to Tranquilize. When used horizontally, line carries the eye across, in an easy, relaxed movement.

This can be translated into:
Furniture arranged horizontally along a wall— to create an illusion of width.
A row of pillows on a sofa to emphasize a horizontal already created by the sofa.
An arrangement of objects in a horizontal line.
A long, single shelf.
One horizontal picture or an arrangement of pictures in a horizontal line.
A window treatment.
Beams in a ceiling.
Furniture of the same height being used together to create an illusion of an unbroken, horizontal line.

An awareness of line is important as a tool, not only to define space but to help create the kind of atmosphere desired within that space—restful, active, peaceful, or busy.

Note the use of horizontal lines in the room settings shown on the following pages.

It Can Shape Space. Looking down on a room, the shape of the spaces formed by the placement of the furniture is easy to identify. How space is shaped does influence the activity and the interaction that takes place within it. (1971 BURLINGTON HOUSE AWARD WINNER "Young Family in Connecticut" submitted by Joanna Brown of Glamour *Photo Courtesy of* Glamour © *1970 Conde Nast Publications, Inc.)*

If there are a number of activities in the room, the space for each can be defined by the lines formed by the arrangement of furnishings, as in the room with the conversation area and study area each facing the fireplace, yet separately defined (page 230).

It Can Unify. With the many diverse areas in a living space being shaped for activity, line can also be used to unify these areas to create a feeling of spaciousness to carry the eye easily from one area to the other, and perhaps even beyond, to the outdoors.

In the open plan apartment shown on page 231, the height of the furniture in both areas is similar so that the eye moves easily from one to the other. The repetition of the verticals in the posts, the chair coverings, and the windows also acts as a unifying factor.

Sensitivity to line is important. Once achieved, it becomes an effective tool in creating harmony within a given area. It means applying knowledge of line to such major decisions as the size and shape of a rug or where and how large pieces of furniture are placed so as to be in harmony with the rug and the lines of the room.

It even applies to minor decisions, such as the arrangement of place mats to follow the lines of the table, and the attention given to the lines of a centerpiece. It is attention to such details that creates harmony within an area as a whole. Some examples are shown on the following pages.

233

form

Form is the definite shape of an object. It usually identifies the function of an object, and the function or basic structure, in turn, may define the form, since the intended purpose of an object will, naturally, influence its form.

Form and shape are really interrelated; the shape of an object is two-dimensional, its form is three-dimensional, and defines the space that the object occupies. In fact, form is the sum of the shape plus the aesthetics of an object.

Notice the forms of each of these objects. They clearly define the function.

Bottom left:
(Courtesy George Jensen Inc., New York)

(Courtesy George Jensen Inc., New York)

Now, notice these forms. What is the function of each?

Both are salt and pepper shakers. The pair on the left clearly define their function. The contents of each can be seen, the quantity available is obvious.

Sometimes form is not logically related to the function for which the object is intended. An objective appraisal of form in relation to function is one way to determine whether an object is well-designed.

Form has been described as "a particular organization of shape, capable of arousing the emotional and intellectual participation of the individual." This emotional experience, in essence, means involvement, an appreciation of the aesthetic qualities of the form, as well as the structural shape. Although shape is an important factor in this esthetic experience, the form's ornamentation or enrichment also plays a role. Some individuals know intuitively whether or not the ornamentation adds to the beauty of a form. How do you feel about the ornamentation on the objects shown on the next page?

(Environment 70 designed by Milo Baughman for Thayer Coggin, Inc.)

237

Opposite page:
(Courtesy Gump's/San Francisco)

(Courtesy George Jensen Inc., New York)

239

If you have some doubts about ornamentation, these questions will help as a guide:

Is it germane to the function?

Does it contribute beauty to the object?

Does it restrict the function at all?

Is the design in harmony with the lines of the form?

Is the size of the decoration appropriate to the form being decorated?

Are color and texture suitable to the function?

Is the design stylized or realistic? Although it is not necessarily a truism, generally speaking, a stylized design—one that reproduces the shape of an object, but does not copy it in detail—is more interesting than one that tries to recreate an object in exact detail. For example, this wall sculpture of stylized birds is far more interesting than the same theme might have been if reproduced in photographiclike detail from nature.

Does the object maintain its dominant character?

Is there diversity within the unity of the total design?

An awareness for form can be developed, just like an awareness for the other elements of design.

The eye can be trained:

To study the form of an object.

To analyze the form in relation to intended function.

To evaluate the aesthetics.

Sometimes the sense of touch can also enter into the evaluation. One can learn to "feel" the form of an object—to develop a sensitivity to form and its relation to function.

241

texture

Texture is the surface interest of an object. It can be actually experienced with the hand, and other parts of the body, or intellectually experienced with the mind. Textures evoke a highly personal, subjective, and emotional response in individuals, much as colors do.

There is a difference between actually touching a texture, and imagining how it will feel. However, an interrelationship between the senses of sight and touch does exist so that it is possible to "feel" a texture by looking at it.

An individual reaction to a form can be definitely affected by the visual or tactile response to its texture. Strongly contrasting textures, for example, can attract or repulse, depending on the textures used together. A fur or fur-type pillow used on a smooth-surfaced sofa might be interesting. The same fur-type texture used as a lining in a coffee cup might be quite repulsive.

Perception of texture can be influenced by light and how it is reflected by the form.

A very smooth and shiny surface may attract attention by the amount of light it reflects.

Very rough textures, on the other hand, may not reflect too much light. They can create interesting contrasts of light and dark and may contribute design interest to an otherwise dull surface.

Texture can enhance an area by:
Providing a contrast for the eye, such as a wool embroidery on a pillow.
Breaking up an otherwise monotonous surface, such as a mirror placed on a wall.
Creating surface interest for the eye, such as the interesting grain of wood, the design on a bowl, uneven slubs in handloomed fabric.
Giving a desired illusion — for instance:
the cozy comfort of a fur throw or rug.
the rich feeling of velvet.
the cool feeling of a glass surface.
Appealing to the imagination, especially a handcrafted object that may not have the regularity of texture that is found in a machine-made one.

A variety of textures used together can add interest to many different types of situations:
Mealtime
The rest area — especially if someone must spend an extended period of time in bed, by choice or by necessity
A work area
An area for social interaction
An area for contemplation

Teapot with hand chasing by Colin Richmond (Courtesy of the American Crafts Council, New York, New York)

A word of caution, however. The use of texture in the home must be thoughtfully planned. Too many textures, used without a sensitivity to the contribution each is making to the situation, may contribute more busyness and activity than is desirable. Some unifying factor such as color, line, or form, and much discretion (sprinkled with trial and error and family response) may be helpful. Also, the aesthetics of a surface sometimes can be harmed instead of enhanced by an attempt to disguise it. For example, if a wooden surface is painted to look like marble, it may give that effect to the eye, but when the hand touches it, the familiar texture of the marble is not there, and the surface loses its aesthetic appeal. An unfamiliar texture, however, need not always be incongruous. It can be imaginative and amusing too.

Perhaps the best way to develop confidence in the use of texture is to experience it and to understand your own personal response to it. The following pages have illustrations that were carefully selected to give you an opportunity to think about your reaction to different textures. As you look at each object, think about the following:

What is your intellectual evaluation of the texture? What is your intellectual response to it?

What is your emotional response to the texture of each object?

Do the textures of some objects give the illusion of being heavier than others?

Do some textures give the impression of being warm or cool?

Do you like some better than others? Which ones? Why?

244

*Bottle and Bowl of Stoneware by Neal Townsend
(Courtesy of the American Crafts Council, New York,
New York)*

246

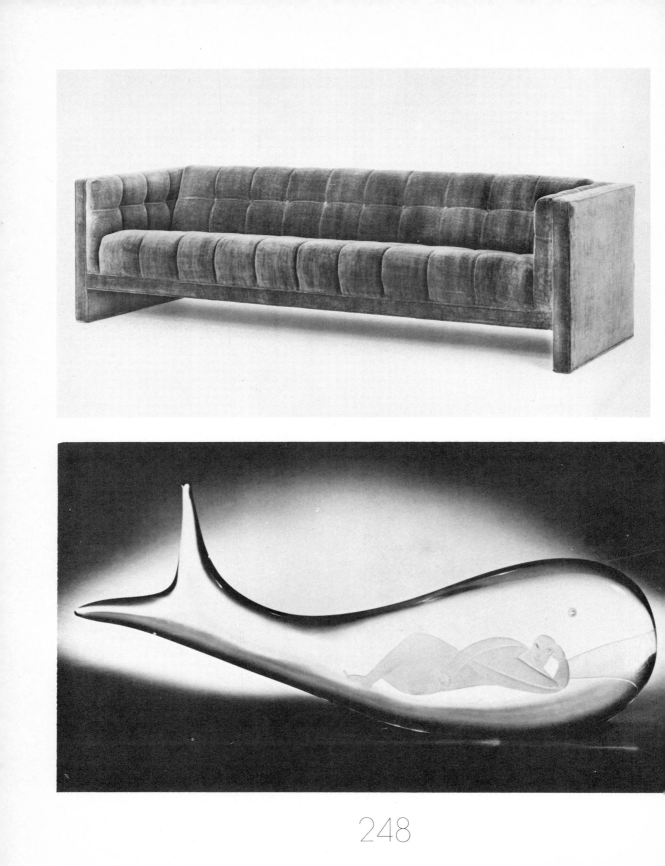

Opposite page top:
(Courtesy Selig Manufacturing Company)

Opposite page bottom:
(Courtesy George Jensen Inc., New York)

(Courtesy Robert Sonneman Associates, Inc.)

"Year of the Dove," primitive double weave by Terry Illes.
(Courtesy of the American Crafts Council, New York, New York)

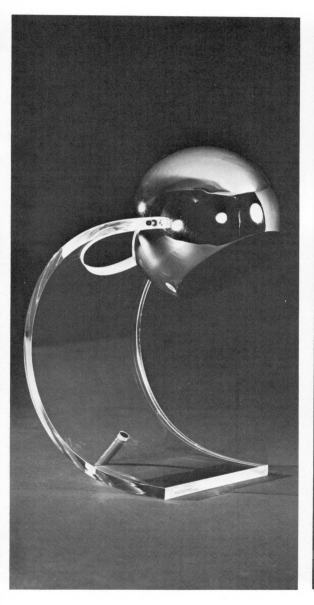

Opposite page:
The rough textures on the walls and ceiling of this room contrast in a charming manner with the textures of wood and fabric of the furnishings.
(BURLINGTON HOUSE 1970 AWARD "Young Family on the West Coast")

There is an interesting interplay of texture in this area for eating. The table itself is rosewood, the placemats are round mirrors set in painted squares, and the centerpiece flowers are silk. The mirrors on the wall, and the translucent vertical blinds break up the wall surfaces with more texture.
(Courtesy Window Shade Manufacturers Association and Brenemen Shades)

Lighting may enhance texture, too, by playing up the contrasts of light and shadow, by adding a depth not apparent at first glance. This brick wall has been lighted by two different types of lighting. Here, it is "washed" by lights that are 28 inches out from the wall and 28 inches apart. The surface appears somewhat flat and reflects light into the room.

To create more of a "feeling" for the texture of the brick, a different lighting technique "grazes" the wall, adding the depth that is apparent.
(Courtesy, Large Lamp Department General Electric Company)

color

Color as an element of design is complex. It is probably one of the most influential factors in the home environment, and one of the least understood. It requires more than a brief mention here, so an entire chapter has been devoted to it later in this book.

However, some aspects of color can be related to making design work in the home.

For example:
Color can influence the apparent size and shape of an object. Dark walls and furniture may make it appear small; light walls and furniture can give an illusion of more

space. This is because light colors recede and reflect light, while dark colors advance and also absorb light. Dark colors will make an object seem heavier than will an exact duplicate in a lighter color.

Psychologically, this can be used to advantage. Furnishings that need to be moved a great deal might be selected in light colors to make the load seem lighter. Or, objects that need to look heavy, might be used in a dark color.

A bright color, repeated around a room, can create a feeling of activity by carrying the eye from one spot to another.

In evaluating the color of a design, whether it is an object, or a given space, these questions should be considered:
Is the color suitable to the form and the function?
Is it appealing to those who must live with it?
If bright colors are used, are they offset by some neutrals?
Does the entire object or space have a feeling of unity of color—not necessarily one color, but a feeling of the colors forming a unified whole?

Generally, the larger the area, the less intense the color should be. The eye may become tired from too much stimulation from vibrating color, although the degree of over-stimulation is very much a personal matter.

In the room shown below, a rich dark brown has been used to unify the furniture and walls in a rather small room. The overall effect is a cozy feeling.
(Courtesy Window Shade Manufacturers Association)

258

Color can emphasize the form and shape of an object by making it stand out in contrast from its background. The bright red sofa in this room is very noticeable. The sharp contrasts in this room, by attracting the eye to individual pieces, make the room *appear smaller.* Sometimes this is desirable.
(Courtesy Selig Manufacturing Co.)

Here in this room color has been used as a unifying factor. The bright red pattern on the many different elements creates a total look, rather than an accumulation of many individual pieces. (Courtesy Window Shade Manufacturers Association)

262

Color can also create a warm or cool feeling. On these pages, note how the room on the left with its reds and oranges has a "warm" feeling, while the one on the right with the blue and the chrome seems "cool".

(Room on opposite page, Courtesy Wallcovering Industry Bureau)

(Room on this page, Courtesy Milo Baughman Communications Workshop)

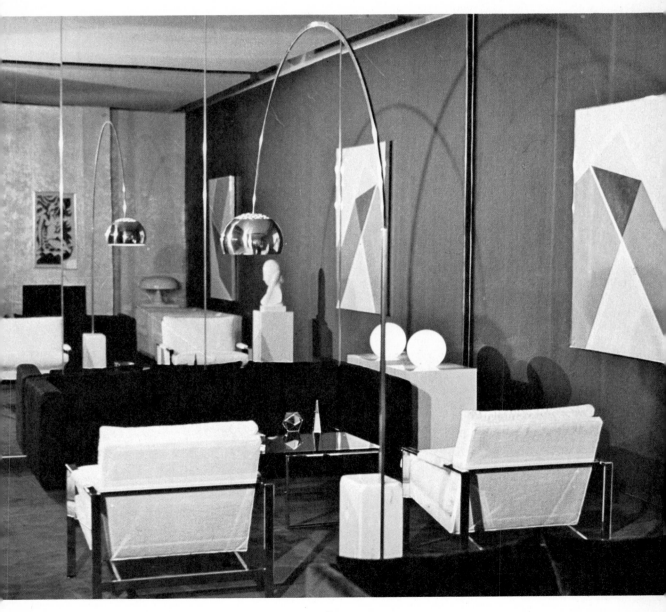

proportion

Proportion is difficult to define and even more difficult to teach in relation to home furnishings. It is the relationship of the parts to each other and to the whole. One does not worry about proportion when an object is made up of two equal parts. Concern for proportion develops when there are more than two parts or when an object is not divided equally, and a judgement must be made about the relationships of the parts.

There are many opinions and mathematical formulas, including the golden section of the Greeks, about how to achieve and define good proportion. But somehow, in the light of contemporary times, these rules seem too arbitrary and confining.

How then can one learn to judge good proportion; how can it be applied to the selection and arrangement of furnishings for the home?

Perhaps, as in the use of color, an experimental approach, based on observation and awareness of the surroundings, can lead to an appreciation for and an understanding of proportion.

Let's start with an observation of proportion in nature:
What is the ratio of the leaves to the stem?
What is the proportion of the plant to the container?

The next step might be to observe some rooms or parts of rooms that seem pleasing and to analyze the proportions of parts of units to the whole.

Looking at the chest and mirror as one unit, notice the relationship of each component to the total unit. How is the total area divided? What proportion of the total is each?

European Fan Palm
(*Courtesy Everett Conklin*)

Japanese Loquat
(Courtesy Everett Conklin)

(Courtesy Fortrel Carpet by Dan River)

Then, to apply what one has learned from observation, it might be well to test personal judgement of the proportions of many different objects, both individually, and in relation to one another. Which of the portions here and on the following pages are most pleasing to you? Do you like some more than others? Why?

Once a basic "feeling" for proportion begins to develop, it will be important to put it into the perspective of why proportion is important in the home. Proportion within an object is important, but what is really more important, is the relationships of proportions to one another in a given area so that a pleasing environment is created.

Again, no rules can be arbitrarily set. Trial and error, an awareness of what makes a pleasing proportion, and a discriminating mind and eye will be helpful in the final analysis.

There are two different opportunities to observe proportion on this wall. To the left of the carved panel, there are three components that can be observed, each in relation to the whole, and to each other.
To the right, the proportion of the fireplace opening can be studied as part of that section of the wall
Design for carved panel at side of fireplace by Mignonne Keller
(Courtesy of the American Crafts Council, New York, New York)

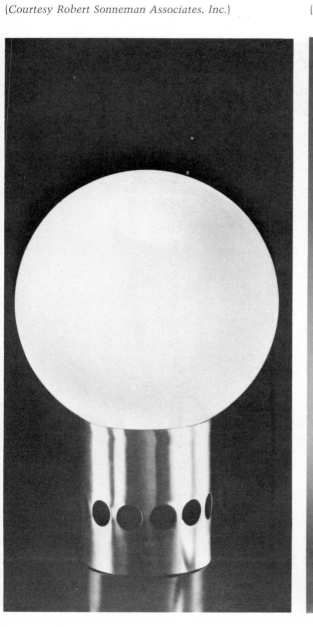 

270

Rocking Chair by Tage Frid
(Courtesy of the American Crafts Council, New York,
New York)

(Courtesy Gump's/San Francisco)

balance

All objects in the home have weight — actual weight and "visual" weight. This "visual" weight, which the eye perceives, is what one must learn to balance to create a pleasing environment.

There are three basic types of balance that can be used to equalize the relationships of weights within an area: symmetrical, asymmetrical, and radial.

One may wish to balance objects, areas, or even one side of a room with another side.

Symmetrical. When the elements on both sides of a center point are equally balanced, it is known as symmetrical, or formal balance, because it actually gives a formal "feeling" to the area. It is a restful arrangement for the eye to enjoy.

Asymmetrical. This type of balance depends a great deal on judgement, since it is the balancing of visual weights, instead of exact objects on either side of a central point. Asymmetrical balance may be achieved by balancing colors, by numbers of objects on one side against a larger one on the opposite, and by what may be two totally different objects that seem to balance each other visually.

The area may not always seem balanced at first glance, because there are not two of everything on either side of a central point. This type of balance is usually more lively and less formal than symmetrical balance.

Radial. Just as the name implies, radial balance is circular. All the elements of the design radiate from a center point (imagined or real). On the following pages a few examples of these three kinds of balance and how they might be used in the home are shown. Once an awareness for balance is developed, opportunities for using it to contribute to an attractive environment in the home will become apparent.

272

On these two pages, furnishings are arranged in symmetrical balance. In the room setting, a commode with a decorative lavabo hanging over it serves as the center point for balancing equally the two lamps and two chairs.
(Courtesy J.C. Penney Company, Inc.)

273

This fireplace mantel is an interesting study in design. Not only are the two porcelain birds symmetrically balanced, but the birds in the painting also seem to be in formal balance with those on the mantle. The repetition of the birds is also an example of the use of rhythm to create unity in design.
(*1971 BURLINGTON HOUSE AWARD WINNER* "*Town House in Washington, D.C.*" *Photo Courtesy* House & Garden © *1970 by Conde Nast Publications, Inc.*)

Here, objects and furnishings are balanced according to visual weights in what are two applications of asymmetrical balance.
In the old Southwestern home, the Mexican "sanctos" on one side of the fireplace mantel is balanced visually, by two candlesticks on the other. Both the picture and the fireplace opening might be considered the center point of the balance.
(1971 BURLINGTON HOUSE AWARD WINNER "Man's Home in Arizona" submitted by Nancy Sortore of the Arizona Daily Star)

In this somewhat more formal room, the sofa might be considered the center from which components in the room are balanced. Visually, the tall cabinet seems to be equal in weight to the chair and table on the other side of the sofa. A similar balance might have been achieved with rather large plants instead of one of the components of the balance.
(Courtesy J.C. Penney Company, Inc.)

Radial balance is seen rather frequently in the home. It may be in little ways, such as the arrangement of cookies on a plate, the numbers on the face of a clock, or designs in textiles.
If a round table is used for eating or other activities, the chairs placed around it form a radial balance. When the table is set for eating, as shown here, the place settings form a radial balance with the flowers in the center as the focal point.
(Courtesy Window Shade Manufacturers Association)

Lighting fixtures quite often are balanced around a central point. This one designed by Robert Sonneman is a beautiful example.
(Courtesy Robert Sonneman Associates, Inc.)

On the opposite page, there is an illustration of a fabric design with radial balance.
(Courtesy Burlington Industries)

rhythm

In everyday life, rhythm is a movement or procedure with a regular recurrence, which can be uniform or patterned. It occurs in nature in the changing of the seasons as well as in the rush of every day living when regular schedules are met day by day.

In design, rhythm is the quality that moves the eye in an organized fashion from one part to the other. It is a matter of forms and lines that divide space into intervals.

Even living plants grow in a rhythm of their own, carrying the eye from the central core to the many parts, while maintaining a unity of design.

When used in the home, rhythm can make an environment stimulating and beautiful.

This may be done in a number of ways:
By repeating a motif, in a continuous line or a predetermined shape. This may add unity to an area as well as rhythm to a design, when a design is repeated in different parts of a room.
By alternating motifs. This method may be more interesting to the eye because, although it is carried along, there is diversity within the unity, and the eye can stop to ponder.
By a progressive change, larger or smaller, in objects or shapes that are being repeated.

Rhythm may be achieved with colors and textures, as well as with lines and objects. When used in the home environment, it can unify different objects in an area, or different areas in a room. It can add design interest to an otherwise dull object; it can be the force to carry the eye from one area to another, creating a feeling of spaciousness.

Rhythm must, however, be used with intelligence. Too much repetition of one motif or object, or color, especially if it is not too interesting, can be dull rather than stimulating, and design that is not interesting in itself can be boring when repeated over and over again, even in an organized pattern.

This extraordinary area reflects the application of rhythm to create a feeling of unity. The diamond motif is used on the floor, walls, and designs on the upholstery. There is much to attract the eye and stimulate the imagination, but it is organized by repetition of the basic motif.
(1971 BURLINGTON HOUSE AWARD WINNER "The Travel Reflection Home" submitted by Denise Otis of House & Garden *Magazine Photo Courtesy of* House & Garden © 1970 *Conde Nast Publications, Inc.*)

281

These Early American quilts use alternating motifs in two quite different applications of rhythm. Both are lively designs which are interesting to look at, with a diversity of pattern that recurs at regular intervals. (BURLINGTON HOUSE 1970 AWARD "The Remodeled House")

Alternating motifs can be applied to furniture, too. Here, the foam chairs designed by Swiss designer Henning Korch have been worked into an alternating red and white arrangement by interior designer Elroy Edson. The wallpaper motif, in a smaller scale also has an alternating motif.
(Courtesy Selig Manufacturing Company)

Opposite page:
*Jack Lenor Larsen has used alternating motifs to create
this mohair and worsted casement cloth.
(Courtesy Jack Lenor Larsen, Inc.)*

*This hand carved door in an old adobe house in Arizona
uses alternating motifs in the overall design as well as
in the center motif.
(1971 BURLINGTON HOUSE AWARD WINNER submitted by Nancy Sortore of the Arizona Daily Star)*

*Repeating the print fabric in two different areas of this
room creates a unified feeling, both in design and color.
(Courtesy Window Shade Manufacturers Association)*

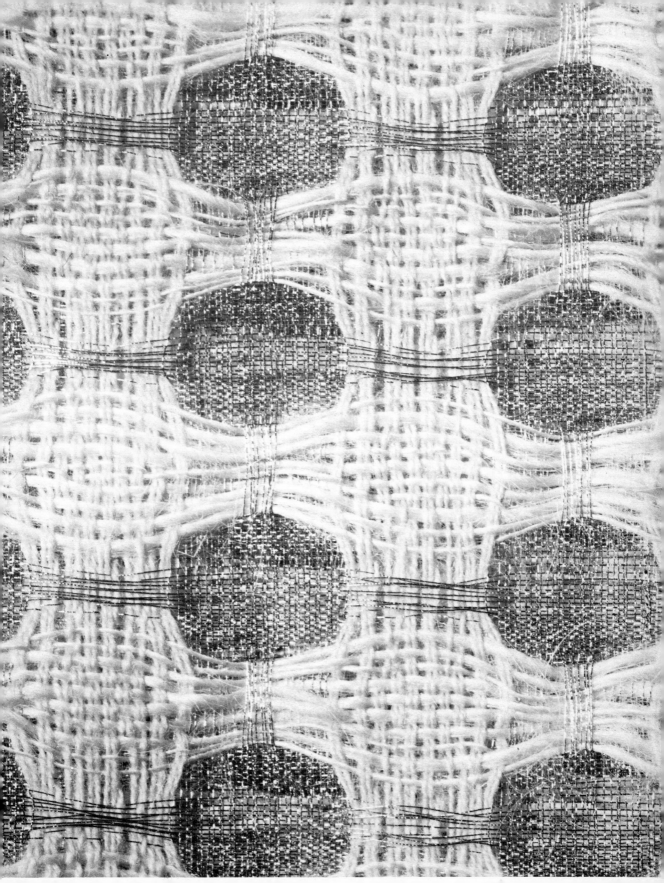

emphasis

(1971 BURLINGTON HOUSE AWARD WINNER submitted by Alison Harwood of VOGUE © The Conde Nast Publications August, 1970)

All elements in an area are not of equal importance. Some are of primary interest or concern; others are secondary. By focusing on an object, or an area in a room, it is possible to emphasize the dominant function.

On the following pages there are illustrations of how the dominant function of a given area has been emphasized. In the first, emphasis is definitely on the bed — which is after all, the prime piece of furniture for the function of the area.
The stark simplicity of the room on the next page draws the eye to the dining table and chairs, and, secondly, to the art.

Following this, in an area for socialization, the furniture is arranged to focus on the fireplace. A secondary emphasis, the piano, is in sharp contrast to the wall and has a small grouping of furniture related to it. In all of these areas, the eye can easily identify the primary function.

Of course, emphasis is not for function alone. It is to add interest, to focus on beauty, to relieve what might otherwise be monotony in a room. It can be created by sharp contrasts in color, prominent designs, a difference in size from surrounding objects, or variation in texture. Lack of emphasis can result in confusion.

The decision about what to emphasize is such a personal one. It all depends on what's important to the individuals making up the family that lives in the home. It could range from hobbies, to art, or to an arrangement of flowers from the garden. It might be a piece of furniture that's been in the family for years, an interesting fireplace, or even a homely but important thing like a wall to display papers brought home from school.

286

(1970 BURLINGTON HOUSE AWARD "Bachelor's Home in the South")

Although the prime function for eating is obvious in this room, a second and important focus is the collection wall to display family treasures.
(1970 BURLINGTON HOUSE AWARD "Young Family in Tennessee")

290

A grouping of pictures and art objects, can make an entire wall an area of focus in the room, and provide sensory stimulation as well. (Courtesy Window Shade Manufacturers Association)

Emphasis need not always be on furnishings. Sometimes furniture can be arranged to focus on an area outside, such as this grouping at the window which frames a view of the outdoors.
(Courtesy Window Shade Manufacturers Association and Joanna Mills)

Application of Design

In a people centered home, an understanding of design can be applied to bring together furnishings that will create an aesthetically pleasing environment, as well as one that functions efficiently.

To evaluate the design elements in furnishings being considered for selection, these questions might be used:

What is its function? To what end use will it be put? Will this object fulfill those expectations?

Do the lines define the function?

What kind of illusion will the lines create: active, restful, vertical, horizontal, busy, or interesting?

Do the lines involve the eye? The mind?

Will the lines of the object help to clearly define a space?

Does it have surface interest? What kind? Do you like it?

What kind of emotional response do you have to the texture? Do you like it, love it, want to touch it? Does it look as though it would be warm or cool? Which effect do you want?

Does the texture create any illusions of weight or temperature?

How important is texture to this object? Should it be an integral part of the design or the important feature?

Is the texture appropriate to the design and function?

How will light affect the texture?

Will the texture require extra care?

Is the color aesthetically pleasing?

Is the color psychologically appropriate?

Is the color functional? Will it be easy to live with over a period of time?

Will it relate to the colors of other objects to be used with it or near it?

Does the color make the object advance or recede? Which do you want?

Is color the most important feature of this object? If so, will it really stand out in the area in which it is to be used?

Does the form define the function?

Is it practical? Easy to clean?

If decorated, is the decoration attractive and appropriate?

Is material suitable to form and function?

If there is a pattern involved:

Is the eye carried from one part to the other in an organized way?

Is the scale appropriate to the form and size? Do the lines follow the line of the form?

Is the color of the pattern pleasing? Interesting?

Are the lines restful? Active? Busy? Interesting? Which is appropriate to the use of this article?

Are the components of the unit in pleasing proportion to one another and to the whole?

Will the proportion of the unit be suitable for the area of the home in which it will be used? Will it be compatible with other items used around or near it?

Although the cost of furnishings and accessories cannot be overlooked in making a final decision, neither can it be measured precisely. Personal values play such an important role. Sometimes an item seemingly costs more than appears appropriate or logical, but if it fills a personal or family need or satisfaction, it may well be worth the price.

If cost is a factor:

What about upkeep? Will it be expensive?

What is its life expectancy? Will you be able to afford to replace it?

Will the cost make it too dear to enjoy if it is breakable or perishable?

Will it have long term value, or is it a passing whimsey?

Is the cost commensurate with the design and the workmanship?

The final analysis, of course, in all of this is: is it appealing to the individual? Will it be suitable for his needs? Will it serve to express individuality?

The questions regarding function and design are important as guidelines in making a basic decision, but ultimately any furnishings for the home must be appealing to those who will live with them.

This raises a question: Should all furnishings in the home be required to meet standards for good design? The answer is obvious. If design requirements are permitted to dominate the needs of human beings, the joy of living in a home is lost.

Some furnishings are selected as gifts by family members. The sentimental value of such possessions, even if they do not meet any of the requirements of good design, is important. So, too, is the psychological value — to the receiver, as well as the giver. A feeling of participation in selecting something for the home can encourage the psychological need for belonging and acceptance; appreciation by other family members of the item selected can encourage self-confidence and can foster family loyalty and pride. The warm glow of love in using an object given by one family member to another can make a task lighter and can help relieve tensions.

Once the decisions about selection of furnishings are made, how they will relate to one another in a given area will be determined to a considerable degree by the basic functional components of the area. The application of design is one of refinement—of defining and shaping the space and of arranging the components so that they are pleasing to the senses and stimulating to the mind.

Defining Space. Some people prefer a feeling of spaciousness, with one area flowing into the other, visually carrying the eye from space to space with no dead ends in view. Others prefer sharply defined spaces, with definite beginnings and endings. The choice is an individual one. However the space is defined, it is application of the concepts of line and form.

There are a number of ways to create a feeling of spaciousness.
Visually or physically, one should be able to move out of one space and into the other, without difficulty. This may be as simple as sitting in a chair and looking beyond the area to a garden on the other side of the window. It may be the easy flow of one area into the other, without too many different shaped forms to block the visual space.
Furniture needs to be small in scale.
The area can be unified in line, color, and design.
Shiny, reflective surfaces, including walls and mirrors will add depth.
Large pieces of furniture may be placed near the walls so that they do not cut space in the room.
Conversely, line and form can also be used to define areas sharply.
The form of a piece of furniture for a particular function will define the area of the activity.

Furniture may be arranged to create a line to define the outer perimeters of an area.
The form of a piece of furniture may define the area of the activity. A desk and chair in place for use for example, define an area for work. A table with chairs placed around it defines the area for eating. One room may have several distinct activity areas, each defined by the forms of furniture used to carry out the activity.

Chairs placed in a grouping for conversation create a line which defines that area. A placemat defines the area for a place setting. Pieces of furniture of the same height, when placed side by side, may create a sharp line that could be used to divide a space.
Color may be used to define areas, too. Space for storage of special equipment may be painted one color. Territory for personal possessions of individuals in the home may be assigned different colors.
Sometimes it may be desirable to visually unify all the furnishings for one activity in an area. This, too, may be accomplished by using the same color on each of the components.
Before any application of information about design can be made, some experimentation may be desirable. Is the space to be flexible? Or permanent? Will the line that's created by the arrangement be restful? or active? which is desirable in this situation? What are the dominant lines in the area? Is it desirable to try to repeat these lines in defining the spaces? Or, is it more desirable to create an interesting definition of space within a given area to achieve the most suitable environment?
On the following pages, a few examples of application of design to defining space are shown.

Because the scale of the furniture in the room to the left seems small in relation to the high ceiling and the size of the room, the eye can easily move from the socialization area to the patio outside, as well as to the room seen through the doorway. All this contributes to the spaciousness of the area.
(1970 BURLINGTON HOUSE AWARD "Weekend Home on the West Coast" Photo Courtesy of House & Garden © 1970)

In the room pictured below, a small area appears to be much more spacious because the furnishings have been arranged near a large window, making it possible for an individual to visually move out of the space to the garden beyond. The outside world has been made part of the inside world.
(1971 BURLINGTON HOUSE AWARD WINNER "Town House in Washington, D.C." Photo Courtesy of House & Garden © 1970 Conde Nast Publications, Inc.)

There's a considerable amount of furniture in this room, but it is all placed to define areas—the socialization area, the eating area, the study area. The height of the two sofas being the same helps to create one unbroken line. The diagonal lines in the rug contribute design interest.
(Courtesy Window Shade Manufacturers Association)

Creating Visual Interest. There are so many different ways to use design to relieve monotony in the home:

Pairs of objects can be symmetrically balanced on either side of a central point to call attention to their likeness.

The structural lines of a room may be repeated in the way that accessories are placed to carry the eye from one to the other, to create diversity within unity.

Supplies and art objects may be grouped together on one wall for emphasis. So, too, can hobbies.

The concept of asymmetrical balance can be applied to arrangements of interesting objects, to create a still life for visual and emotional enjoyment.

Variety in texture will appeal to the sense of touch as well as to the eye.

Visual unity can be achieved by repeating a color, a design motif, or a texture.

Color may be used to emphasize an art object, either by sharp contrast, or as an interesting background.

One of the most frequent ways in which visual interest is introduced into the home environment is through pictures. How and where they are hung is as much an emotional matter as it is an objective one, since personal enjoyment is one of the important factors.

So many of the concepts of design can apply to how and where pictures are placed.

One large picture, or a grouping of pictures over a single unit of furniture will create an area of emphasis.

Sometimes an entire wall can become an important point of emphasis in a room when it is hung with pictures.

For either of these uses, some guidelines can be helpful. To be effective, the outside perimeter of the pictures should follow the lines of the area being filled, and if hung over a piece of furniture, the lines should also relate to the unit of furniture.

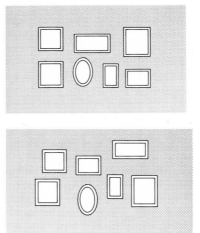

Some other considerations:
Balance within the composition is important. Visually, "heavier" pictures such as oils, used with "lighter" ones such as water colors need to intersperse so that the entire

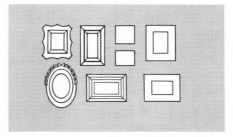

302

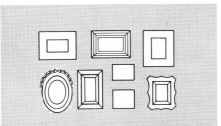

Placing large pictures on either side of a grouping and placing smaller ones within the unit will create a more pleasing balance, than hanging heavy ones together and small ones together.

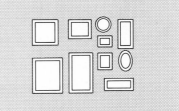

unit is balanced. Otherwise, the composition seems divided, with one side "weighing" more than the other.

This applies to sizes of pictures, too. Too much space between pictures destroys the rhythm of the arrangement. A general guideline to remember is that the distance between pictures should not be greater than the height of each picture.

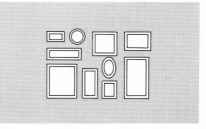

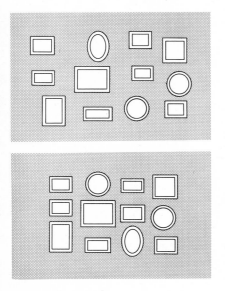

Proportion is important, too, in the relationship between pictures and the wall area where they hang. The size and shape of the wall area and the size and shape of the pictures needs to be compatible.

For example, pictures on a rectangular wall space will be in pleasing proportion when they are rectangular in shape or hung to form a rectangle.

Pictures hung over a rectangular unit, such as a chair, table, or small chest should follow the shape of the furniture and be in pleasing proportion to it. Above all, the arrangement must not seem top heavy.

one already used in the area (rhythm), to tie together several colors used in the room, or to introduce color as a form in the room.

On the following pages there are many ideas for putting an understanding of design to work in creating an interesting environment in the home. The individual elements have been explained on previous pages, and examples of how they could be applied in the home shown. However, in practice, planning an environment may involve a multiple use of these in any given situation.

Although the ability to express self in one's environment is not dependent on a knowledge of the various concepts of design, a working understanding can be a useful tool to help individuals fulfill the need as described by Fromm "to feel the creator, to transcend the passive role of being created, to express individuality, and to create a setting that helps meet man's basic craving for beauty."

One of the most effective ways to use design in day-to-day living is the area most often neglected with the attitude that it is not necessary for the family. This is the area of foods, and decoration for festive occasions.

A few extra minutes spent in arranging food attractively can transform an ordinary meal into a visual delight, Almost any of the concepts of design can be applied.

A helpful rule of thumb to remember in deciding on proportion is that the area between the unit and the bottom of the picture frame should not measure greater than the length of the frame of the picture.

Pictures may be used to emphasize line in an area, or to carry the eye from one area to another. They may also employ color to repeat

To the left, the structural lines of the room are repeated in the placement of the old tools, to emphasize the design interest. Note, too, the asymmetrical balance used in placement of paintings.
(Courtesy Mr. & Mrs. Theodore Donahue)

The storage unit in the room pictured below, which groups everything on one wall, makes a handsome point of emphasis in the room. The objects stored in it may be grouped within sections according to various design concepts, as well as the principles of storage.
(Courtesy Window Shade Manufacturers Association)

Design concepts can be applied to small areas as well as entire rooms. Here, using the small painting on the easel as the center point, the objects on either side form an interesting asymmetrical grouping on a table top. (1971 BURLINGTON HOUSE AWARD WINNER "The Ski House" Photo Courtesy House Beautiful © *1970 by Hearst Corporation)*

There are so many textures to be enjoyed in this room—leather, wood, velvet, steel, plastic, mirrors, and fur. The variety creates visual interest in the room, helps make a stimulating environment.
(Courtesy of Selig Manufacturing Company)

The horizontal stripes of the fabric used in the shades and pillows of this room are repeated in the design over the fireplace to create visual unity in this small area. (Courtesy Celanese Fibers)

*A number of design concepts have been used to create
visual interest in this area.
Emphasis—the large painting
Rhythm—alternating pillows
Balance—lamps and tables on either side of the sofa
(1971 BURLINGTON HOUSE AWARD WINNER "Town
House in Washington, D.C." Photo Courtesy of* House &
Garden © *1970 by Conde Nast Publications, Inc.)*

Here is another example of the use of emphasis to create interest. This time an entire wall has been hung with many pictures, held together visually as a unit, yet each distinctly unique, offering variety within unity. (1971 BURLINGTON HOUSE AWARD "Do-It-Yourself Home" © 1970 Meredith Corporation)

A "cozy" room uses generous amounts of velvet—a texture that creates a feeling of warmth. The furniture is arranged in a form that creates an enclosed area for people to relate. There are a number of horizontal lines (which give a restful feeling) in the table, the long picture over the sofa, and in the continuous line formed by the sofa tops. (1971 BURLINGTON HOUSE AWARD WINNER "Young Family in Brooklyn" submitted by Joanne R. Barwick of Modern Bride Magazine)

313

With a little extra effort and an understanding of how to use design effectively, foods for two different occasions have become a visual treat. Both are examples of the use of radial balance in arranging foods.
(Tea setting courtesy Tea Council of U.S.A., Inc.)
(Cake courtesy General Foods)

This setting below is an interesting use of rhythm. The motifs on the cake repeat those on the glasses and napkins. On the cake, alternating squares of plain and pattern are still a different application of rhythm. (Courtesy General Foods)

The precise beauty of this setting for an oriental meal, when studied closely, is an excellent example of rhythm. Not only do the like pieces of food form a pattern that carries the eye from unit to unit, but the lines of food also repeat the lines of the straw mat underneath. (Courtesy General Mills)

The strong horizontal lines in this living room are restful. The built-in furniture not only repeats this line but, by concentrating seating along the wall, creates a feeling of spaciousness. The proportion and scale of the furniture is appropriate to the room also. All add up to a peaceful environment.
(*Courtesy Dr. Verda Dale*)

A room with many lines, vertical, horizontal, and diagonal, keeps the eyes busy. So, too, do the different textures and the many points of emphasis. (1971 BURLINGTON HOUSE AWARD WINNER submitted by Alison Harwood of VOGUE © Conde Nast Publications August, 1971)

319

By the very presence of a pool, this area gives the impression of coolness. The minimum of furniture contributes to the psychological impression of a cool, calm place, with lots of uncluttered space, and no busy lines in furniture or wall coverings to distract the eye or the mind.
(*1971 BURLINGTON HOUSE AWARD WINNER "Town House in Philadelphia" submitted by Barbara Barnes of the* Philadelphia Bulletin)

A New Approach to Color

"Color is a basic human need, like fire and water—a raw material indispensable to life," said the painter, Fernand Leger. Psychologists would describe it as the need for sensory stimulation.

The color explosion of recent years has brought about a new point of view on how to use color and where to use it. Color is seen everywhere—pastel colors in balloons and flowers, bold colors at major expositions, in stores, playgrounds, and even in the kitchen; whimsical colors are used in ads and labels; restless reds, oranges, and violets are used by the young to match the tempo of today's rock music. Some would maintain that people today need restless colors to keep pace with all the environmental stimuli in everyday living.

Somehow, this bold new use of color has made the familiar concepts of color theories seem too confining, and the long-held "rules" for combining colors seem to belong to a world of yesterday.

The new trend toward more freedom in the use of color also incorporates a new approach to using color—for its sensuous impact. Color has become an important tool for self-expression, and to be successfully used, it must be approached with the freedom to experiment, to try new ways to use colors—together and alone.

Many artists today compose colors to create the sensuous impact desired. Some use maximum contrast, others use very little contrast. Color is used to create an impact. It is the material from which the form is created, instead of imitating the color in an already existing form.

To learn a whole new attitude toward color is not an easy task, especially if the "rules" for combining colors have been a formidable barrier. Perhaps the place to start is with the rules themselves, to learn how different societies have used colors for symbolism and how these colors will differ from one group to the other, so that the "rules" really do not hold.

In the traditional Chinese theater, these color symbols have been used:

Yellow, worn by the emperor, empress, and crown prince.

Red and blue, worn by the good people. Red means loyalty, blue means ferocity.

Black, painted on a mask means integrity and white means deceptiveness.

Although not adhered to much today, tradition in Bangkok called for certain colors to be worn on different days:

Yellow on Monday.
Pink on Tuesday.
Green on Wednesday.
Orange on Thursday.
Blue on Friday.
Mauve on Saturday.
Red on Sunday.

In Morrocco, the Arabs paint a bright blue on one wall of their houses to keep away the evil spirits.

The American Indians also had their own system of color symbolism.

The Pueblos used colors for the different directions of the compass:

North was indicated by yellow.
East was indicated by white.
West was indicated by blue.
South was indicated by red.
Up and down was indicated by varigated or black.

The Cherokee Indians had their color symbolism for the compass, too, which included predictions:

North signified blue and trouble.
East signified red and success.
West signified black and death.
South signified white and happiness.

In ancient Egypt, colors that occurred frequently in dreams were also interpreted as symbols. For example:

Black meant the death of someone close.
Bright red meant ardent love.
Dark blue meant success.
White meant happiness in the home.

In our own society, certain preconditioned ideas about color prevail:

Red used in a traffic-light means stop; it can also mean danger.
Yellow means wait; green means go.
Red and green used together symbolize Christmas.
Red, white, and blue together are patriotic.

Some people think red is a hot color to wear, perhaps because it is associated with fire.

Colors are also used to describe people and their emotions:

Green with envy.
Purple rage.
Yellow—lacking in courage.
Blue—a depressed mood.

Most people undoubtedly will have some prejudices and cultural symbolisms within their frame of reference regarding color. There is nothing wrong with that, as long as one can recognize them for what they are, and can go on from there to develop an awareness for color.

Color is everywhere in the environment—sometimes in man-made settings:

In Buildings and historic shrines.
In posters.

324

Courtesy Communication Workshop

In native crafts.

In toys.

Sometimes in natural settings:
In a bright red and yellow fire hydrant against
  green grass.
In a weathered wooden building.
In a growing plant.
The face of an animal.

To develop a sensitivity to color, planned color experiences are important. A deliberate attempt must be made to learn to look for color, to "open one's eyes" to see color where it has never been seen before, to become aware of how it is used, to develop a "feeling" for it.

The objects pictured below are not rare—they are a part of most individuals' experiences. A first quick glance can easily identify the colors of each. But take a closer look. "Open your eyes" to the color variations within each object.

Now look at the pictures on the next page—they are all one color. Or are they? "Open your eyes" again—notice the subtle differences.

As a consciousness for color develops, old inhibitions about "rules" for combining colors may gradually begin to disappear.

The important thing to remember about using colors is the sensuous impact they can make. This is a very personal reaction; it will differ with each individual, as it should, if color is to be a personal experience.
Courtesy Communications Workshop

Now, consider the color combinations here and on the following pages. What kind of reaction do you have to each? Your reactions don't have to be profound. They may be as simple as "I like" or "I don't like," or they may be more emotional. It's a very personal thing.

After you have decided your reactions to each, "open your eyes" and look at each combination more critically. Study the colors used together. Do some of them relate to preconceived color notions? Do some represent new groupings of colors that you would not have thought about before now? Why did you like some and not like others? Are you beginning to get a "feeling" for color?

Once this "feeling for color" begins to develop, it's not too difficult to begin using color with a new freedom.

Actually, this experiencing of color on a personal basis can be an exciting approach to learning about color. It is learning through doing. It encourages discovery: of what is important to you, of how you feel about different colors, of the kind of colors you might like in your home environment.

It does not guarantee confidence in the use of colors at first try, but with experience it can lead to insight into their impact on you.

The warm monochromatic colors of an old weathered door on this page may be translated into a noncolor setting of a room, such as the one on the facing page. Courtesy Communications Workshop

Now that you have studied the colors used in rooms on the previous pages, do you have some understanding of what colors and color combinations are more appealing to you than others? Are you developing some confidence about your own color judgments? Actually, ideas for combining colors do not need to be completely original. There are many resources all around, as we have seen, in nature and in man made surroundings. They can be translated into colors for the home, not literally, but in the mood and spirit they convey. Some examples are shown here and on the next few pages. Note the general feeling each combination of colors creates.

The first attempt at translating an idea may be a feeble one, but there has to be a beginning somewhere, sometime. It might be the translation of an interesting color to an idea for a room. It might be a mood expressed with color in the spirit of a room; or even a direct and literal repetition of colors seen somewhere.

Black and white are often seen in graphic displays. They can be the perfect background for experiments with color — starting with inexpensive accessories, such as paper flowers, all the way to trying a new color in a chair.

As you look at these pictures, once again, study your preferences and test your judgment. Which ones do you like best? How would you have translated the ideas and moods if you had been creating these areas?

331

The colors in a popular advertisement may become the basis for colors for a room.
Courtesy Communication Workshop

A poster serves as inspiration for developing a color plan for a room.
(Reprinted by special permission of LADIES' HOME JOURNAL © Downe Publishing Inc.)

The sunshine colors of nature can help to create a
cheerful room.
Design by Milo Baughman for Thayer Coggin

*Beiges and off-whites might become a relaxed environ-
ment—one that can seem both warm and cool—as the
light changes.
Design by Milo Baughman for Thayer Coggin*

Bold colors, which a few years ago may have seemed too much for use in a large area, may be surprisingly serene.
Design by Milo Baughman for Thayer Coggin

Courtesy Communication Workshop

Colors, of course, are not seen alone. They are experienced in multiples. It's the impact of the multiples that creates the mood, the sensuous effect desired.

Consider these multiples:

What feelings do you have about each group of multiples? Which ones would you want to use in your environment? How would you use them?

Are there some you would change in composition? How? What feelings do you want to create in your environment? How would you use color to create these feelings? Which colors would you group into multiples?

Now look at these room settings. What kind of mood does each convey to you? What impact do the colors create?

In planning the home environment, the impact of color must be considered in relation to the entire family as well as to the individuals within it. Their needs as well as their personalities will influence the role color plays.

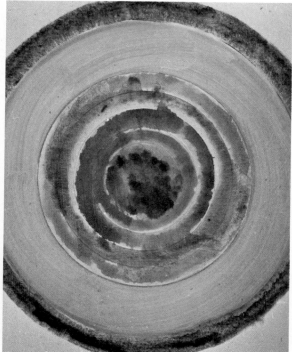

Is the family active or quiet?

Do family members like constant stimulation?

What role does home play — is it a quiet refuge from active lives individuals have outside the family? Is it a place to stimulate activity? To relieve boredom from outside activities?

Do family members entertain friends at home? How often?

Is the family traditional?

Is there a spirit of adventure in the home? If so, is it limited to some family members? Which ones?

Is there room enough for individual expression with color? If not, what opportunities can be created for individual involvement in color decisions?

For some families, making a decision about color in the home may not be an easy one. Personal preferences may be strong. Approaching the problem, however, from the function and mood color will help to create, may put it into perspective. The decision then does not become one of which color to use, but how to use colors to create a given impact, or sensuous feeling to an area in the home, and which colors will best achieve the effect desired.

Although the impact of a color or a given multiple of colors is the prime consideration, some practical factors must be considered, too.

These generalizations about color may be guides to use, along with the new freedom with color, to make it work effectively.

Color, itself, is neither traditional nor modern. How and where it is used determines the impression it conveys.

In any room, color is used in the plural. Even an all-white room contains numerous shades of white.

Color patterns may be influenced by how one color is used in a pattern. For example, a green and white print, a green and white stripe, and a green solid, even though they use the same green, will give a plural effect of greens, because of the interplay of the green and the white in each design.

Wood tones, the shine of metals such as brass, steel, copper, and other materials such as glass or marble, all contribute to the color in a room.

A room's entire mood can be changed, just by changing the accent colors.

The use of white and off-white on walls and floors will create airy, spacious rooms. Light colors will tend to make a room larger, while darker colors will create a more compact feeling. However, contrasts must also be considered. An object that is in sharp contrast to its background will be prominent in a room. Therefore, a light-colored room with draperies and furniture in sharp contrast will appear smaller, instead of larger, because each of the objects will stand out, will attract the eye, and will break up the continuity of the background. In order for the room to appear larger, not only must the background be light but the furnishings should blend with it. This does not mean that all small rooms must be treated with light colors, or all large ones with dark colors. The choice is a personal one. Some people might like a small room to look even cozier with dark colors.

In a small room, one color on the walls and furniture will create a less cluttered, calmer effect.

Broken into patterns, bright hues create a more gentle effect. For example, a bright red might be intense in a solid area. The same color, broken up into pattern with white surrounding it, would be less intense and more subtle.

When a bright color is a favorite one, but its use in full intensity seems overpowering, using it broken into a pattern may create a satisfactory compromise.

By changing the intensity (degree of purity or strength) of a color, its position can be softened or strengthened in a room. A chair covered in an intense colored fabric, for example, will be more dominant in a room than one that is a pastel color.
Warm colors will make a piece of furniture appear larger, and cool colors will make it appear smaller.
Because cool colors can make an object seem smaller, they can also create the impression of being farther away.
One bright bold color, such as orange, a sharp yellow, green, or a bold blue, spread over a large area of a room with comparable areas of white, can create a pleasing setting that will not overpower the people in it.
A room saturated with a deep color can be neutralized with wood tones and bright white accessories.

Visual Illusions Are Important Considerations, Too. Color has a visual impact as well as an emotional one. How it is used and what other colors it is used with will influence what the eye finally sees.

Consider these effects carefully. Starting on this page and continuing on the next few, there are a number of exercises planned to

help you "see" the effect of colors on each other.

Simultaneous Contrast. Background colors affect foreground colors in unexpected ways.

Both arrows are the same shade of gray. Notice the difference in appearance of the gray, however, against the two different background colors.

339

Simultaneous Contrast. Although this is a continuous ring of the same color gray you can change its color by placing your finger or a pencil along the line separating the red and the blue. The two light-blue colors appear to be different, but are actually the same color ink.

Contrast Stripe Effect. Colors on a nonuniform background are subject to many unexpected changes. They will tend to change in the direction of the lighter brighter colors or darker duller colors surrounding them.

The blue bars in this illustration are all printed with the same color ink. Notice how the color of the blue changes as you look at it from different angles.

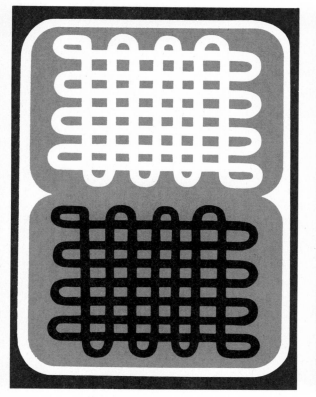

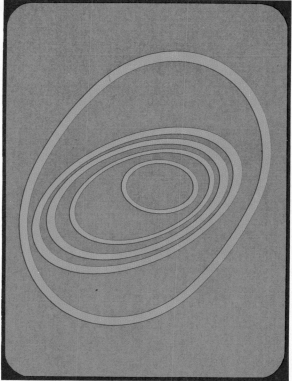

Spreading Effect. Divide the illustration in half by placing your finger or a pencil between the black and white grills. The red behind the black will appear to be a different color than the red behind the white.

Vibration. Look steadily at this illustration. Complementary colors of equal lightness and high saturation have a tendency to make each other appear more brilliant. To some this is a visually disturbing effect.

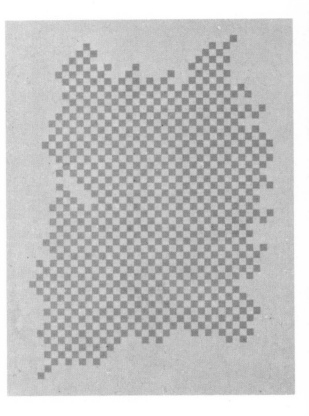

Spots Before Your Eyes. Stare at the checkered pattern. Flicking gray spots appear as you glance at it. Try to look at one particular gray spot and it disappears.

Additive Special Fusion. Alternating squares of yellow and blue are seen at reading distance. At a viewing distance of approximately 25 feet the yellow and blue squares will become fused into a uniform gray.

Advancing and Receding Colors. The red wall at the end of the hall seems closer than the blue wall. Red is an advancing color; blue is a receding color.

Negative Afterimage. Stare for half a minute at the black dot in the green heart. Then look at the black dot on the white screen. The pink hearts you may see are the negative afterimage.

What Is Color? Since Sir Isaac Newton first analyzed light, scientists have had various theories on the phenomenon of color, but all are based on established principles.

Colors are actual wavelengths of energy radiating from the sun. These waves vary in length, creating the different colors in the spectrum. They can be clearly seen when the waves of radiant energy strike a glass prism. Each wave is a different length. The longer waves (red, orange) bend the least; the shorter ones (blue, violet) bend the most, so that the light comes out the other side of the prism as separate waves. The human eye sees them as red, orange, yellow, green, blue, and violet. The colors of the rainbow repeat this same color sequence. White light contains all the colors of the spectrum.

Scientists agree on this basic definition of color. They differ only in their ideas of how best to break down these main colors into the whole range of possible color gradations.

Dr. Wilhelm Ostwald, a physical chemist, grouped colors according to hue, each equidistant from the other around a circle. His objective was to identify colors, and he did break them down into 24 separate distinguishable colors.

The Goethe Color Triangle arranges nine basic colors to show the relationship of primary to secondary to tertiary colors.

Schopenhauer experimented with color to determine the relation and balance of light with quantity within the color wheel.

Albert Munsell, an artist, developed his system to categorize colors by hue, chroma, and value. This, too, was intended for the identification of colors so that those using color could accurately communicate with each other when describing colors.

However, many have attributed to these systems, as well as to others that have also been developed, absolute authority for how colors should be combined and used.

This is where the frustration about color rules hinders creativity. All these color systems play an important role in the function they were originally designed to fulfill—that of identifying colors and their relationships.

An in-depth study of all of these theories is not essential to understanding how to use color in the home. For the professional who plans to use color intellectually to achieve certain effects, a working knowledge of the various color theories can provide a foundation from which to work and to experiment.

Individuals as well as families can use color with more confidence if they can approach it from a personal point of view. This must start with experiencing color, learning to "see" color and how it is used everywhere in the environment, gaining insight into self by discovering what colors and groups of colors are most pleasing. Then, gradually, developing an understanding of how colors relate and how they interact, one can build a working knowledge about color that can be applied to creating the kind of environment needed for each individual situation.

How Is Color Experienced?

1
The sun radiates energy in the form of wavelengths. Sunlight contains all the colors of the spectrum, and each color is expressed by wavelengths within a certain range.

3
The eye registers the reflected color on the retina. The rods and cones in the eye define the shape and color of the object by transforming the radient energy into chemical energy which, upon energizing nerve endings, sends impulses to the optic nerve.

2
The light source (sunlight or artificial) reaches the object; some light rays are absorbed, some reflected, depending upon the colors in the light source and the color of the object. Only the reflected light is seen by the eye.

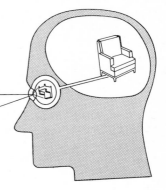

Man mixes colorants which will selectively absorb or reflect specific hues in the light rays.

4
The optic nerve registers the message and sends it to the sight center of the brain. It is at this point that the individual becomes aware of the color of an object.

Many factors influence the color of an object:
The way the object absorbs, transmits, or reflects the light waves striking it.
The surroundings of the object.
The physical condition of the viewer's eye.
The psychological association of color concepts with the object.

But, perhaps, the most important factor is the light source under which a given object is seen. Objects are visible to the human eye only because light from them enters the eye. Without light, objects could not be seen and, in turn, without reflected light, colors would not be possible.

The color in the light source must be reflected off the object in order to give back the color of the object. When looking at a piece of red fabric under white light, the red color is reflected most—all the other colors in the light source are absorbed by the red fabric. In turn, a white fabric looks white because it reflects all the colors in the light.

The type of light outdoors is sunlight, which contains all the colors of the spectrum. It is usually stated that daylight is white, but sunlight is scattered by the earth's atmosphere and thus the type of light is changed by the time of day and condition of the atmosphere.

The rising or setting sun contains more red and will cast a reddish glow on all objects. A hazy day produces a bluish light—often families find this color unpleasant and turn on incandescent lights within a home to cast a yellowish glow.

The light from an incandescent lightbulb is white light, but it has a larger amount of red and less of the other colors. Fluorescent lights have more blue. Different colors are seen when an object appears in different kinds of light.

For example, a wall that is white under a white light can be made to appear red when it is lighted with a source that is predominantly red. Actually, the wall will only seem to be red because only red wavelengths of energy are being reflected from the wall to the observer's eye.

The Psychology of Color.* Psychologists have found that the emotional impact of color tends to lead to outwardly directed action. A knowledge of this fact combined with research on how human beings react to certain colors has been applied successfully in industry, hospitals, and schools to influence performance. This knowledge can be applied to the home, too. For example, common reactions to some colors have been found to be as follows:

Red, exhilarating, stimulating to the brain, pulse, and appetite.
Pink, festive.
Yellow, energizing, creates sense of well-being.
Green, soothing, refreshing, nature's color.
Blue, serene and relaxing.
Gray, noncommittal, reduces emotional response.
Purple, enigmatic, shade and texture affect color.
Raw Red, overstimulating.
Intense orange, increases tension and irritates.
White, neutral, neither stimulates nor calms.

* "Color—a Many Faceted Tool," *Penney's Forum*, Spring and Summer 1968.

Color Family	Light Source	Effect of Light Source on Color Family
	Natural white fluorescent	Makes all these colors appear rich, clear and vibrant
	White fluorescent	Gives a yellow cast to lighter shades—fades and dulls the darker shades
	Warm white fluorescent	Makes light shades clear and bright—gives a slight yellow cast to brighter reds—a slight brownish cast to darker reds and rusts
	Deluxe warm white fluorescent	Makes all these colors appear bright and rich
The Red Family	Soft white fluorescent	Gives a pinkish cast to all these colors— intensifies reds
	Deluxe cool white fluorescent	Gives all these colors a clear, cool appearance —slightly darkens some of deeper shades
	Cool white fluorescent	Greys and darkens most of these colors
	Daylight fluorescent	Greys, deadens, or gives a violet cast to these colors
	Incandescent	Gives an orange cast—makes most of these colors rich and glowing
	Natural white fluorescent	Darkens these colors giving them a slight grey cast
	White fluorescent	Makes these colors bright and clear with a slight yellow cast
	Warm white fluorescent	Makes lighter shades bright and clear—darker shades deep and warm
	Deluxe warm white fluorescent	Makes these colors deeper, richer, warmer, with a slight yellowish cast to the lighter shades
The Green Family	Soft white fluorescent	Greys, or gives a bluish cast to these colors
	Deluxe cool white fluorescent	Makes these colors clear and light
	Cool white fluorescent	Greys all of these colors, darkens yellow-greens, clears blue-greens
	Daylight fluorescent	Brightens, clears, gives a blue cast to all of these colors
	Incandescent	Darkens all of these colors, giving them a yellow or brownish cast

Color Family	Light Source	Effect of Light Source on Color Family
	Natural white fluorescent	Makes all these colors appear clear, rich and bright
	White fluorescent	Makes green-blues greener, lighter shades clearer—greys darker shades
	Warm white fluorescent	Makes all of these colors richer, lighter, clearer
	Deluxe warm white fluorescent	Warms and deepens most of these colors
The Blue Family	Soft white fluorescent	Greys or gives a slightly violet cast to most of these colors
	Deluxe cool white fluorescent	Makes all of these colors appear lighter
	Cool white fluorescent	Slightly greys or darkens all of these colors
	Daylight fluorescent	Makes all of these colors appear cool, bright and very blue
	Incandescent	Gives a yellowish or greenish cast to most of these colors—dulls or darkens the deep colors
	Natural white fluorescent	Clarifies, brightens, makes all of these colors warm and rich
	White fluorescent	Lightens and warms most of these colors—gives a yellowish cast to cocoa and grey shades—greys mauve and rose tones
	Deluxe warm white fluorescent	Enriches and brightens all of these colors
The Pinks and Tans	Soft white fluorescent	Brightens and deepens these colors, giving a reddish cast
	Deluxe cool white fluorescent	Makes these colors appear warm, clear and rich
	Cool white fluorescent	Greys and darkens all of these colors
	Daylight fluorescent	Greys and dulls these colors, giving a slight blue cast
	Incandescent	Gives an orange cast, makes these colors bright, rich, warm

Color Family	Light Source	Effect of Light Source on Color Family
	Natural white fluorescent	Subdues these colors somewhat
	White fluorescent	Gives these colors a clear yellow cast
	Warm white fluorescent	Brightens and gives a warm, soft yellow cast to all these colors
	Deluxe warm white fluorescent	Makes these colors appear warm and deep with a slightly orange cast
The Yellow Family	Soft white fluorescent	Deepens and gives these colors a pinkish-brown cast
	Deluxe cool white fluorescent	Enriches, clarifies and warms most of these colors
	Cool white fluorescent	Slightly greys and darkens most of these colors
	Daylight fluorescent	Dulls, greys and darkens all of these colors
	Incandescent	Warms and enriches these colors

^a The information in this chart is from "Color Is How You Light It," courtesy of Sylvania Lighting Center, Danvers, Massachusetts (*Penney's Forum* Spring/Summer 1968).

Bright, warm colors tend to condition most people for action — toward outwardly directed interests and muscular activity. Whereas soft, cool colors are conducive to introspection and mental tasks.

Research shows that people react to color in many ways and that their reactions may be expressed with both physical and psychological responses. These responses are observed with red, blue, and green particularly. For example, when a room is predominantly red there may be an increase in blood pressure, a quickening of muscular responses, a general feeling of restlessness and emotional excitability, and a tendency for time to drag. In contrast, the blues and greens may tend to slow muscular response, to calm the nerves, and to cause people to underestimate long periods of time.

What Colors Do People Prefer? Even the most skilled color specialist could not use color effectively without a knowledge of color preferences. Preferences, as they relate to color psychology, have been studied in many ways. However, most studies have been done with small samples of relatively high color purity in red, orange, yellow, green, blue, and violet; variations in color, texture, the specific item, and the like, would need an infinite number of samples. The research reports show relatively little variation in their findings. In general, people seem to prefer cool colors to warm colors, with the order of preference usually listed as blue, red, green, violet, orange, and yellow.

Colors choices have been studied with relation to age, sex, intelligence, education, socioeconomic level, and biological influence.

349

The results of studies have revealed few significant relationships but show many interesting trends. Children's choices change with age and tend to move from warm to cool colors. Other studies indicate that as age, education, income, and exposure to color associations increase, so does the tendency to select subtle colors with little contrast. Color choices seem to be closely related to affections and acquired learnings.

It will be interesting to observe whether today's young generation, which sees so many bright colors in clothes, toys, classrooms, and the brightly colored environment, will have a different attitude toward color preferences in the future. Certainly, they do not suffer from sensory deprivation as far as color in the environment is concerned.

The psychological importance of color cannot be underestimated. Persons living in severely controlled environments, who have experienced the absence of sensory stimulation, sometimes become psychotic or create a dream world of their own. Even zoos today are building more colorful environments, since it has been found that the life span and reproduction rate of its animals increase in this type of environment.

Functional Color. The psychological factors about color can be used to make it a functional tool.

Some examples where it has been used successfully are:
A European hospital used blue in the surroundings of patients with high blood pressure to relax them and red in those of patients with low blood pressure to give them a feeling of stimulation. Yellow was used for patients with mental trouble, since it creates a sense of well-being.
Dark colors can make an object seem heavier than can light colors. When two identical packages are painted two different colors, one dark and one light, the dark will appear heavier to lift. In an industry where much lifting of heavy packages is necessary, the packages will be planned in light colors to make the lifting seem lighter. Sometimes moderately heavy equipment such as sewing machines or vacuum cleaners are manufactured in light colors so that they will not seem so heavy to move. Conversely, some products such as clocks or radios, which may be small, are sometimes made in dark colors to make them appear heavier.
In children's hospital wards, intense colors, such as bright pink, turquoise, and yellow are used to create an atmosphere of mild "pandemonium" to help children keep their minds off their illnesses and their aloneness. These exciting colors seem to have a beneficial effect when combined with care from nurses and hospital aids. These same colors used for adults in hospitals would irritate them.
Yellow has been found to have the greatest visibility, so it is used for school buses and many taxies. In industry, it is used on machinery projections and low beams.
Color is used in offices to facilitate organization and communication between departments, to visually define where papers belong. For example, all communications going to department X might be planned in a bright pink envelope and those going to department Y in a bright green one. Or, carbons of letters that are typed may be dif-

ferent colors — white for the file copy, yellow for the follow-up action, and pink for circulation to others who might be interested.

The same information could be applied to the home.

In a bedroom shared by two sisters, color could be used to identify each person's furnishings. This helps contribute to a sense of belonging and security, one of Maslow's hierarchy of needs.

In the bathroom, individual colors can identify trays of grooming aids, towels, and a storage drawer for each family member. A chest with different colored drawers might also be used in a kitchen or family room to store hobby supplies or games. Each color could be used to identify the contents. Young family members could then learn to store items by learning, for example, to put toys in the blue drawer, papers in the yellow drawer, and so on.

Color may also provide a safety factor, especially in the bathroom. The top shelf of the medicine cabinet might be painted red for those medicines that must be used with discretion or might be harmful to young people.

Safety can be encouraged by using color for easy identification throughout the home.

In the final analysis, translating color ideas and inspiration into reality is a very personal matter.

It depends on these factors:

An awareness of color and how it works.
A free use of imagination.
A self-confidence in using color.
Self-awareness.
The willingness to experiment — to stray from the "tried and true," the familiar, and the safe combinations.
A recognition that all attempts may not be successful — that they may be used as guides to improving performance.
A recognition that one's concepts about using colors will change with experience, with time, and with one's changing values.

Most of all, it depends on a new approach to color, free from rules — with one important objective — to create an environment for each individual family to relate to in meeting human needs.

SOURCES OF INFORMATION

"Color — a Many Faceted Tool," *Penney's Forum,* Spring and Summer 1968.
"Hailstones and Halibut Bones," Mary O'Neil, *Adventures in Color,* Doubleday and Company, Inc. Garden City, New York, 1961.
Light and Color, TP 119, Large Lamp Division, General Electric Company, Nela Park, Cleveland, Ohio.
"Open Your Eyes to Color," a presentation prepared for the J.C. Penney Company by Communications Workshop, Provo, Utah.
Sloane, Patricia, *Color: Basic Principles and New Directions,* Studio Vista: London; Reinhold Book Corporation: New York, a subsidiary of Chapman-Reinhold, Inc.
The Color Tree, published by Interchemical Corporation, 1965.*

351

Relationships

One of the most crucial understandings in applying all of this knowledge about design to creating a home for people, is *relationships*. It is possible to know all about design elements, and to apply them to individual objects or isolated problems with success, but the real key to the successful use of any of the concepts about design or color is knowing how they *relate to one another*, since it's what each contributes to a unified whole that makes up the total environment. A color may be beautiful unto itself, a gem to enjoy, visually and emotionally, but how will it look when placed next to another color? Will it be enhanced? Will it reflect or take on color from other objects around it? How will this, then, affect its appearance?

The same holds true for all aspects of design. Objects selected individually may fulfill all the guidelines for good design. It's what happens when they get home and are put into use with others that makes the difference.

The familiar mathematical equation about the whole being equal to the sum of its parts applied to the relationship of furnishings in the home really boils down to awareness for details, both in objects and in entire areas.

The Japanese have mastered this awareness into an integration of everything with everything. One leaves Japan charmed by its beauty without quite knowing how to define it. They plan and calculate every detail carefully so that everything used will look well against all other things seen at the same time. No object can be judged or selected until one knows where it is to be seen, and with what other things it will be used. This integration of all details may even include the clothing and manners of the human being moving in front of it. For example, when food is to be served, the right colored dish is chosen to bring out the color and texture of the food. But this is only the beginning. The color of the tray and the color and texture of the other dishes on the tray must also be selected carefully to set each other off, not to match. The dishes must be worthy of the food they will hold. The final form is a poetic statement somewhere between functional requirements and an understanding of the potentials and limitations of the materials used.

The Japanese have four levels of systems by which to measure beauty.

Shibui. This type of beauty is never obvious. It is understated and seems simple, although it can really be complex, because the viewer must involve himself with the object to discover its depths of beauty. It may be a plain fabric that reveals subtle designs when studied carefully, or the individual parts of a garden discovered one by one after the whole has been enjoyed and appreciated for its beauty. The depth of variety and beauty is there, but it is subtle and must be discovered by the individual.

Shibui is the most desirable value in beauty for the Japanese.

Miyabi. This form of beauty is deliberate. Its elegance and splendor can be taken in and appreciated at once. Objects that are miyabi may be rich in appearance with gold or mother-of-pearl inlay, intricate patterns, or they may require great care.

It was originally developed by the aristocrats in the Heian Period (794–1185) when a small section of the society could afford a luxurious standard of living.

Although miyabi means rich, it does not mean excess. It is a highly disciplined sophisticated elegance.

Two examples of miyabi are:
The white tabi worn by Japanese women.
They are impractical because they soil easily and must be changed several times a day, and laundered, but they are charming and beautiful.
Gardens with intricate patterns worked out in sand are miyabi. They are beautiful, but require much care and daily raking to maintain their design — so they are a beautiful luxury.

Hade. This means brightly colored, with many colored combinations. It can be relatively inexpensive like paper decorations for festivals, or a very expensive bridal kimono. It carries no connotation about intrinsic values.

Iki. This is the area for personal expression, but different from Western ways, because the beauty is personalized *within the framework of Japanese tradition.* All details are still planned with care, but modern practical ways may be used to create them or to carry them out. An Obi, for example, may be arranged with personal originality, but still it remains within the tradition of the Japanese.

In the Western culture, there is no such measure of specifications for levels of beauty. Perhaps a little borrowing from Eastern cultures along with a more deliberate effort to think through the interrelationship of everything used together or seen at the same time can serve to emphasize the importance of details in creating beauty in the environment.

Awareness for the integration of everything with everything can be achieved in a number of ways, the most intangible of which is personal taste. One person, carefully selecting those items that reflect his concept of beauty and good design will probably, without consciously thinking of it, select units that

This antique lacquered Japanese lunch box is 150 years old. It is a beautiful example of shibui, with subtle intricacies of design that become apparent only as one begins to examine it more closely. The simple square box comes apart piece by piece to reveal all the components for a meal, including bowls, boxes to hold foods and utensils, and two individual trays.

Not only do the individual pieces fit together perfectly, but even the individual design motifs, (and there are three distinctively different ones) match up on the individual pieces inside the unit as well as outside.

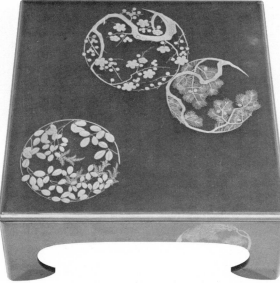

357

will harmonize. Intuition can play a role here. So can sensitivity to design. Some people seem to be naturally attuned to it.

For someone who is just beginning to develop this awareness, a formal framework for evaluation can be the basis for developing confidence in relating furnishings. Before each object is added to an area, it might be considered in the light of these questions:

How will it be used?

Where will it be used?

Will it be near, on, or in front of another object?

How does it relate to other things to be seen at the same time:

In color. Is the color already used in the area? If so, will this repeating of the color enhance its use, or will it become too much repetition of one color? What color will be next to it? How will they look side by side? What other colors will be in use near it? Does it introduce a totally new color in the area? If so, does this add design interest or accent?

In texture. What is the texture? What psychological effect does its texture give? Is it desirable for the area in which it will be used? Is it compatible with the textures of other objects around or near it? Is this texture new or has it already been used in the area? If it is a repetition, is this desirable?

In scale. How does its proportion relate to other objects around or near where it will be used? Will it be in pleasing proportion to the furnishings it will be used with? Is the scale appropriate to the dimensions of the room? To the form of the area?

In form. What are the basic lines of this object? How do they relate to the lines of other objects? Are they compatible with the overall lines of the room?

Is there decoration or a design of some kind on it? If so, will it be a pleasing addition to the area where it will be used? What are the basic lines of the decoration? How many other decorated objects are there nearby? Will they all relate in color and line? Is there a danger of too many different styles or decorations?

How Will It Relate to People?

If it is to be used, is it functional to operate? Is it fragile? Does it require careful handling? Is it to be enjoyed visually or physically? Will it be pleasing to look at?

Recently, there has been a growing trend toward individualism in furnishing homes. This has been indicated by the combining of units from many different sources, the breaking with the traditional "period" rooms, and by using different periods and styles to create a home unique to the individual family. Perhaps this trend reflects the need for individual expression, a reaction to rapidly advancing technology, or maybe it reflects a maturing of our society: a recognition of the worth of the individual, a self-confidence that does not need to hide behind the "correctness" of rooms that follow rules.

Whatever the reason, the trend is a good one, for it recognizes that *Homes are for People.* To be successful, thought must be given to how the furnishings relate to each other as well as to how they express individual likes. The same framework of questions for evaluating an object to be used in an area can be used for an entire room, too. Actually, eclectic

358

Texture, form, and proportion all relate in the furnishings of this informal room. The scale is light and airy, the wicker not heavy, and there's not too much design to compete with the pattern formed by the reeds in the furniture. The room looks comfortable and cool, a perfect setting for a warm day.
(Courtesy J.C. Penney Company, Inc.)

rooms do not usually take shape all at once, anyway. They are the sum total of individual objects and seem to evolve as each new object is acquired.

One of the interesting challenges in planning such rooms is the combining of the old and the new, the antique and the contemporary.

Old furnishings serve a real purpose in many of today's homes. They are the "roots with the past" that provide the psychological security to balance the mobility and tension of the fast-paced lives of many. Sometimes these old pieces are literally family heirlooms, other times they are acquired antiques. It doesn't matter which. The fact that they represent continuity from a day prior to this one is a real psychological comfort to some people. "Marks of time" such as scratches and dents just make them that much more intriguing to the imagination and provide an opportunity for interaction between the object and the person admiring it.

Remnants from childhood are another form of security in the home because they are reminders of a carefree time when as an individual one did not have responsibility for material security and had no major decisions to make. Nostalgia for this state is normal and, according to some psychologists, good because any tangible link with one's childhood encourages a sense of continuity with one's personal past that helps to stabilize and enrich the present.

Some antiques may have such personal significance that lack of design relationship to the room seems irrelevant. The emotional satisfaction becomes the most important factor. Others, however, can be selected with an eye to how they will relate to everything.

362

Another area in the Donahue home where individual antiques have been combined in such a way that each complements the other, to make one coordinated total. Even the shadow of the windows framing the sunshine repeats the lines in the area.

Part of the charm of an eclectic room is the variety that meets the human need for sensory stimulation. Variety need not be limited to styles of furnishings in the room.

It may be as simple as the placement of accessories to create interplay with light and shadows as the sun moves through the day; or it may be artificial lighting planned to create interesting shadows. The concept of holiday decorations, which are used for a brief period and stored away for awhile, might be applied to furnishings, especially accessories, in the room.

Individual expression in creating rooms has many implications. To begin with, home is considered an extension of self. "People frequently see home as an outer shell of self. How he lives determines the view he has of his role, his status, and his style of life." *

Psychiatrist Harold F. Searles suggests that the actual importance of the nonhuman environment to the individual is so great that he dare not recognize it—that it is a conglomeration of things outside the self and an integral part of the self.

If home is to be an extension of self, then one must understand himself to the degree that is possible. A measure of self-confidence and a positive self-concept helps, too. No one formula can be given to help individuals achieve this. Each human being is a unique combination of environment and experience and must find his own answers. Some of everyone's feelings are definite, some are in conflict

with each other, and still others are undiscovered. This exercise has been planned to help individuals gain insight in planning a home that will be an extension of self.

What Is the Real You Like?
If you could plan the interior of a home in any way you like to reflect the *real* you, how would you do it?
How do you feel your best friend would think you would do it?
How would your mother think you would do it?
How would your father think you would do it?
If you are married, how would your spouse think you would do it?

Now think through the furnishings in your present living situation:
What furnishings are *not* the real you?
How would you change them?
What is preventing you from changing them?
Have you clarified your own values about the role of your near environment (home)?
What is your concept of beauty?

One's concept of beauty is a very personal matter. Individual and family values and goals, as well as cultural background all play a role in defining it. So, too, does time. As individuals grow, develop, and change, so also do their concepts of beauty and self-expression. Recognizing this change as a normal process can be a key factor in understanding self, and expressing self in the home.

Beauty in the home can and should be an emotional experience—one that involves the individual—that helps lift thoughts from everyday matters to the whole high world with wonder—that brings peace of mind and soul, and a release from tensions.

* James E. Montgomery, "Impact of Housing Patterns on Marital Interaction," *The Family Coordinator*, July 1970, pp. 267–274.

This is quite a formal room—in texture, line, and design. The woods are rich in color, the fabrics fine and smooth, the lines of the furniture reflect a formal elegance. Even the details of the accessories repeat this elegant formal feeling, and all components relate well to each other and to the whole.
(Courtesy J.C. Penney Company, Inc.)

The rather massive design of the chair and plant stand seem appropriate in proportion and texture to the rough finish of the wall.
(Courtesy of Robbins Products, Inc.)

365

366

Somehow, the plaid of the wallpaper and the primitive design of the cabinets and chairs seem to go "hand in hand." Both are informal, strong in "character" and balanced in scale.
(Courtesy Wallcovering Industry Bureau)

The relationship of food to the dish in which it is served is an important detail in planning an environment for people to enjoy.
(Courtesy General Foods)

Traditional and modern, velvet and stainless steel,
contemporary art and oriental designs have all been
combined quite successfully in this room. Certainly,
personal style and taste combined with an eye for
detail and a knowledge of design played an important
part.
(Courtesy Selig Manufacturing Company)

A spiral Japanese paper lantern, 15th century Peruvian waco water jugs and Le Corbusier's classic modern furniture all seem to belong together in this window corner of a room. The relationship is pleasing. (Courtesy Window Shade Manufacturers Association and Joanna Mills)

SOURCES OF INFORMATION

Gordon, Elizabeth, "Esthetics," one of a series on 32 *New Views of Japan*, Published by Japan Air Lines.

"How to Measure Your Nostalgia," *House & Garden*, November 1962.

Lemkau, Paul V., M.D., "A Psychiatrist's View of Housing," *Proceedings: Seventh Conference for the Improvement of the Teaching of Housing in Home Economics Land-Grant Colleges and State Universities*, October 30 to November 2, 1963. University Park, Pennsylvania, College of Home Economics Publication No. 180, Pennsylvania State University, 1964.

Montgomery, James E., "Impact of Housing Patterns on Marital Interaction," *The Family Coordinator*, July 1970, pp. 267–274.

"Which Is The Real Me?" Penney's *Forum*, Spring/Summer 1969.

ALTERNATIVES
FOR
A CHANGING
SOCIETY

The recognition of home as an important environment for human growth has been slow in coming. More research is needed to gain insight into how human needs can be met in a changing society. More knowledge is needed, too, on life-styles and how they influence personal growth.

Up to this point, this book has dealt with the family and home in the traditional sense. But technological advances on the horizon offer alternatives for the physical environment of the home. The familiar concept of the nuclear family is also being challenged.

Some predict changes in family patterns as we now know them, with a number of alternatives open to individuals. They suggest that early marriages and longer life spans will create undue pressures on individuals; that a marriage time span of almost two generations may be too long a period to expect two people to live and grow together with the many individual experiences to which each will be exposed. The result may be the emergence of a pattern of divorce and remarriage.

Dr. David Cooper in *The Death of the Family* suggests that "the age of relatives is over because the relative invades the absolute center of ourselves." He would like to see a more durable form of commune life.

The commune as a household for individuals to live in together may well become another established institution in the not too-distant future. It may be the way some people choose to cope with the impersonal technology of the times.

Actually, the Latin derivative of the word "family" means "household," not the father-mother-child-connotation commonly acknowledged.

Still other novel family forms discussed are

group marriages, "professional" parents, single parents, geriatric group marriages, and temporary relationships.

With the advent of equal opportunities for women, even the dynamics of the nuclear family as we know it may experience subtle changes. With less emphasis on traditional male and female roles and more emphasis on individuals as human beings, there may be a new focus on human needs and values.

Advances in technology will offer still more alternatives for the home and its furnishings in the years to come. It is predicted that by the year 2000, 77 percent of the nation's population will live on 11 percent of the land. Projections for housing needs for the next 30 years include a recommendation by the National Committee on Urban Growth that 100 completely new cities each with a population of 100,000 people be constructed, plus an additional 100 new cities each with a population of 1 million. If this recommendation is carried out, and if the predicted population increase occurs, it will take care of only 20 percent of the increased need. The actual need is for 75 million new homes.* Construction costs, land costs, and limited availability of skilled labor make the conventional approach to home building inadequate. New concepts in housing are needed. Some are in the design stage now, others have been tried successfully.

One approach is the mobile home. This in-

* *Challenge of the 70's*, a presentation by Joseph Carriero, Chairman, Department of Design and Environmental Analysis, New York State College of Human Ecology, Cornell University to Illinois Chapter, National Home Fashions League.

dustry, which applies factory production methods to housing, has been successfully offering a housing alternative to those who want a home within a limited price range for some time.

Modular housing, a newer concept, offers the possibility of applying mass-production technology to urban housing needs. Usually there are two kinds of modules—a wet one which includes all plumbing, heating, bathroom, and kitchen equipment, and a dry one for less complicated areas in the home. A number of manufacturers are experimenting with this idea, but perhaps the best known modular system is *Habitat* built in Montreal Canada for Expo 67. It is a prototype of city dwellings of the future.

Each unit or "home" is prefabricated at a site not too far from where the housing unit will be assembled. It includes the plumbing, wiring, kitchen, and bathroom units, linen closet, bathtub and sink, and the roof. A crane lifts the unit in place. Each unit rests on another in such a way that the roof of one becomes the terrace of the unit above. These identical units can be grouped to form homes ranging from three to seven rooms.

Somewhat similar in principle is the sectionalized house. It, too, is prefabricated, but the prefabricated units form a single-family dwelling instead of a housing unit for many families. The construction system includes maximum factory fabrication of major subassemblies, ready accommodation of field tolerances in site erection procedures, and the opportunity to please a wide range of user tastes through arrangements of components and materials applications.

The home shown here was designed by FAMILY
CIRCLE working with architect Walter Brown. It com-
bines the know-how of mass production used in mobile
homes with the concept of modular units. Called the
1971 Mobile Modular, it is all plywood and arrives at
the sight in three units (indicated by tone on floor plan)
which are joined together around a courtyard. The total
space in the home is 1500 square feet. A feeling of
spaciousness is created by clerestory windows and floor
to ceiling windows as well as a curved panel roof. The
dining room bridging the living room and kitchen feels
larger than its 11' × 11' dimensions because of its glass
doors leading to the deck on one side and the open
court on the other.
(Art work for floor plan courtesy of Charles Reiger,
Columbia University School of Architecture)
(Photography: Vincent Lisanti. Arrangements for the
above: courtesy FAMILY CIRCLE)

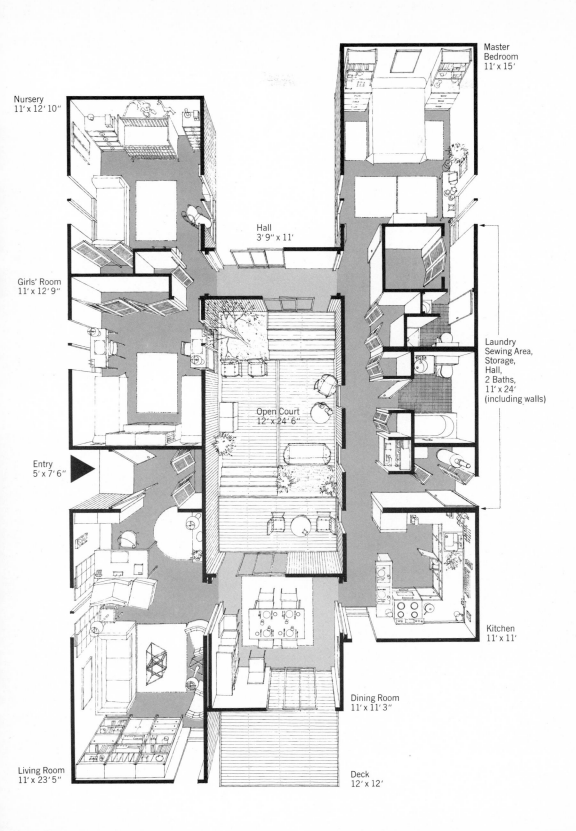

Nursery
11' x 12' 10"

Master
Bedroom
11' x 15'

Hall
3' 9" x 11'

Girls' Room
11' x 12' 9"

Laundry
Sewing Area,
Storage,
Hall,
2 Baths,
11' x 24'
(including walls)

Open Court
12' x 24' 6"

Entry
5' x 7' 6"

Kitchen
11' x 11'

Dining Room
11' x 11' 3"

Living Room
11' x 23' 5"

Deck
12' x 12'

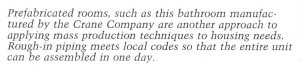

Prefabricated rooms, such as this bathroom manufactured by the Crane Company are another approach to applying mass production techniques to housing needs. Rough-in piping meets local codes so that the entire unit can be assembled in one day.

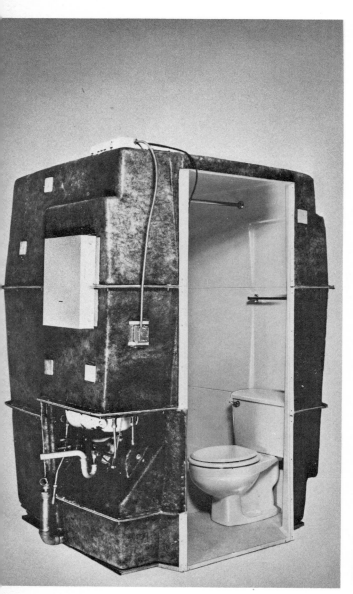

The sequence for assembly of General Electric's pre-fabricated house is shown below and on the pages that follow. Subassemblies typified by the ten shown in this illustration are erected and joined in the sequence suggested. Especially noteworthy are the geometrically plane subassemblies 4, 5, 8, and 9. They provide opportunity to accommodate all tolerances in "closing" the system into one set of contiguous surfaces. They further permit variations in fenestration or materials selection.

Implicit in the handling of these subassemblies is the superior racking qualities of stressed-skin sandwich floor systems, and one-piece castings of major plastered wall surfaces. Factory dimensional control is possible by the use of steel framing. User-preferred treatments in wood have been reserved for surface applications, thereby conserving this valuable and fleeting national commodity. (Courtesy, General Electric Company Re-entry and Environmental Systems Division)

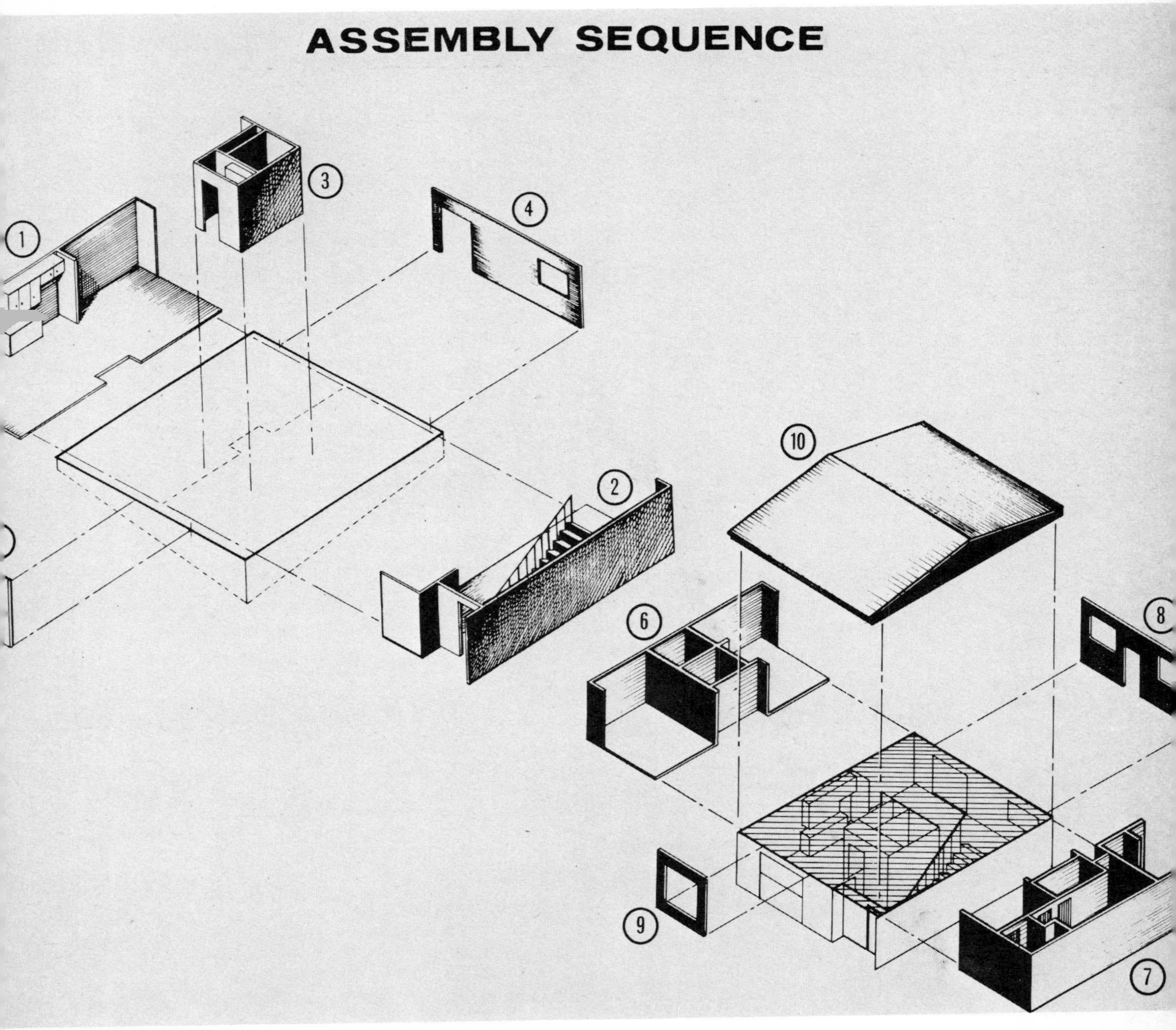

ASSEMBLY SEQUENCE

Here, a utility core for a townhouse is being lowered into place at George Air Force Base, Victorville, California. Kitchen cabinets are attached to left-hand wall, around the corner from air conditioning equipment. This utility core module was manufactured in a nearby factory and transported to the building site for erection as part of a 200-family housing project. (Courtesy General Electric Company Re-entry and Environmental Systems Division)

This is the completed factory-built modular townhouse
at George Air Force Base, Victorville, California.
(Courtesy General Electric Company Re-entry and
Environmental Systems Division)

I BEDROOM APARTMENT   2 BEDROOM APARTMENT   3 BEDROOM APARTMENT

These series of illustrations have shown a number of different approaches to creating new housing using the concept of prefabricated modules. They seem to offer the potential for individual variations even though they are mass produced.

Still other imaginative alternatives to meet housing needs are also being proposed.

Sir Hugh Cassen, head of the School of Interior Design at London's Royal College of Art, visualizes a portable home unit, self-contained for a time, which could be plugged into a parent "tree" for refueling and essential services. He calls this the Diatom House. This house could be capable of living in, on, below, or above land, sea, and air.

"It may be virtually self-contained and self-servicing for short periods, or it may, when staying longer in position, hang with neighbors like dates on a sort of palm tree, which provides essential plug-in services like water, climate, light and waste disposal.

It may be fitted with all sorts of such necessary devices as automatic house and body cleaning equipment, food dispensers, climate machinery, communications gear for ears and eyes, and automatic controllers for moving furniture partitions, even perhaps dissolving outer walls and windows. All the machinery and equipment is out of sight within the double-shell walls. The area is zoned with living, eating and sleeping areas grouped around the dispensing-disposing-storage service core. Extensions temporary or semipermanent, clip on outside as required." (*Home Furnishings Daily*, April 11, 1967.)

Buckminster Fuller envisions his geodesic dome to enclose entire communities, permitting total climactic control. Air could be continuously cleaned and regenerated, thus eliminating current air-pollution problems.

Advances in technology will make an impact on how people live inside the home, too.

Plastics promise one of the greatest opportunities for innovation. Rigid urethane foam is being used experimentally to create interior architecture and even to create furniture by spraying layer upon layer of foam to form shelves and seating units. The design possibilities are limitless: a complete living unit with furniture and area dividers could be made into one structure by using urethane foam.

At the Yale University School of Architecture, an experimental multidomed urethane foam house was created to study the potential of this material for housing.

Terrance Cashin has designed an orb chair from urethane foam. Shaped like a ball, it is 5 inches thick and has a 26-inch internal void so that it can adapt to any seating position at any point.

Inflatable furniture, already on the market, will probably be more commonly used. For a mobile society, it's practical. It is estimated that six boxfuls will hold the furnishings needed for one home.

A practical solution to the problem of dust in the home promises cleanliness without drudgery. A new "positive pressure" technique raises the air pressure in the house slightly above what it is outside. When a window or door is opened, this pressure will keep the outside air from coming in, thus stopping air-bourne dust before it can get inside the house.

There are new uses forecast for electricity,

too. It will be used for "heating with light." The heat released by lighting fixtures will supply most of the heat needed in the home. Heat will be picked up by the room air flowing over the recessed lighting fixtures and distributed where needed. Light will then really be the by-product of heating the home, and the home will probably be illuminated by day as well as by night.

Plastic fibers will be used to transmit light from a central source to remote locations such as drawers, clocks on the wall, the front-door bell, or even a shelf. It will work in the same way as a pipe carries water. This system is known as fiber optics.

New uses for lighting are already here. Furniture is now being designed which incorporates light into the form, so that sofas, tables, and beds become luminous pieces whose bulbs can be changed to provide different color effects as well as light. In fact, changing the color and mood of an entire room is possible by the use of translucent plastic panels equipped with florescent bulbs.

A colored cover can be slipped over a bulb to achieve the color desired. The amount of light can also be adjusted from bright and lively to a soft intimate mood.

Luminal artists are using light alone or with such light-conducting materials as acrylics to create a form of light sculpture. The artist Ronoldo Ferri predicts rooms with no lamps at all—just lighted furniture, black plexiglass walls, and luminal paintings.

Some artists produce programmed movement of sculptured shapes around stationery colored lights to create drifting strokes of color that flash and float across a screen. This type of light art is planned to appeal to the senses, to encourage purely sensual messages.

The living room in the soft-edge foam house contains mostly built-in furniture, all foamed in, of course. To soften the seating units, which are bench-like, and to provide variety in texture, cushions are covered in cotton duck and pillows in terry, cotton duck and stretch denim as well as urethane fabrics.
(Courtesy West Point Pepperell)

These are new furniture forms which incorporate lighting within the unit. The potential for how this concept might be used in creating an interesting environment for people will depend on the imagination of those who live with it. The sofa and table shown are two of many pieces.
(Courtesy HOUSE BEAUTIFUL)

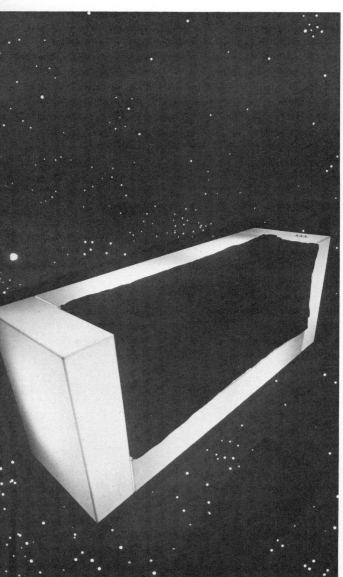

These new concepts for how light can be used in the home open entire new vistas for individualized environments.

Just as imaginative are the ideas being projected by appliance manufacturers.

The Whirlpool Corporation has designed a modular kitchen concept for the future that will permit flexibility in planning and rearranging food-preparation areas to meet individual needs, and to satisfy the human need for variety. It is made possible through appliances that are housed in cubical units that are on a pedestal, and it has been named the "Tic-Tac-Toe kitchen."

The mobility of the units is achieved by having plumbing and wiring available at several different locations around the floor and walls of the food preparation area.

Each small circle on the floor conceals the connections for the utilities. By merely lifting off the cover circle, one can drop in the pedestal of the appliance and the cubical unit automatically plugs into the utilities.

A button or foot lever raises or lowers the appliances, which are hidden in each unit.

In one section of the food preparation area there is a computerized "read out" panel that enables an individual to check the inventory of household items such as clean clothes, meals, individual foods and beverages, paper supplies, and linens.

The computer also has a direct connection to the local supermarket and various supply stores that allows it to do the family shopping when the inventory runs low.

A special electronic washer has also been designed that analyzes the wash load and determines the proper water temperature, detergent, and agitation cycle for the kind of soil in the family laundry.

Still another concept for the food-preparation areas is a compact freestanding unit called "Cuisine 80" by Elkay.

This unit incorporates:
A computer that stores recipes.
A closed circuit TV that monitors other areas of the home.
A stainless steel sink with disposal.
A ceramic pastry board.
A cook top controlled by computer.
A chopping board.
Water temperature control.
A ventilation system in an overhead hood.

It concentrates all food preparation in one compact area, so that the traditional concept of a food-preparation area is no longer necessary.

The Philco-Ford Corporation has developed a "House of Tomorrow" that will offer revolutionary new electronic approaches to meet functional needs.

In this home of the future, rooms are six-sided, providing a wide variety of floor plans and choices of access from room to room. Each room will be prefabricated, prewired, and prefurnished to specifications at the factory.

The house will have a fuel cell for its major power source and extensive wireless communications with the outside world. Telephone lines and water and sewer pipes will be eliminated.

But the most revolutionary aspect will be the use of a central computer that will control all systems within the house. The freedom of design offered by microcircuits — tiny chips no larger than the head of a pin, yet containing an entire circuit — will make possible an electronic complex that will control automatically all lighting, entertainment equipment,

This is the "Tic-Tac-Toe Kitchen" designed by the Whirlpool Corporation. The covers of the small circles on the floor can be lifted to receive the pedestal of the appliance. A close up shows the pedestal being inserted in the circle where it is then connected into the utilities. (Courtesy Whirlpool Corporation)

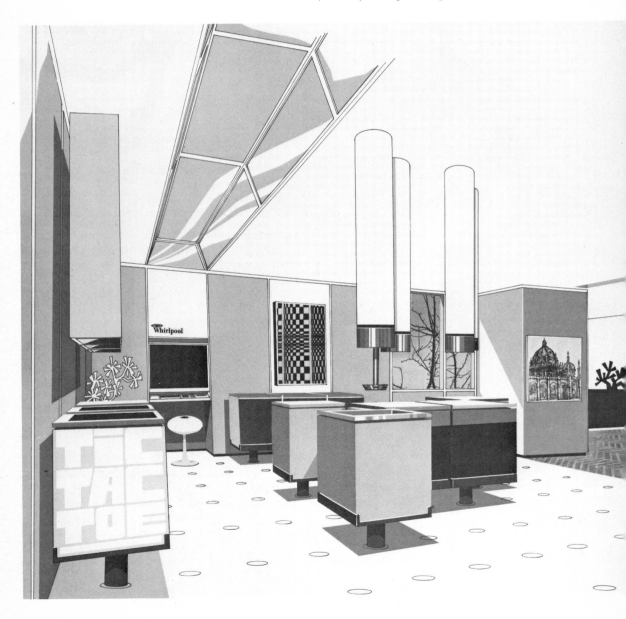

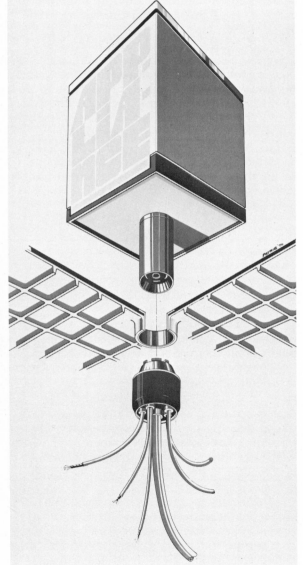

The "Cuisine 80" unit pictured below, which concentrates all food preparation activities in one area, was described on the previous page. *(Courtesy* HOUSE BEAUTIFUL)

389

appliances, and communications gear in a space no greater than that needed for a contemporary portable radio.

The family computer will check the hundreds of electronic circuits required in the house every few seconds, switch to a backup circuit if trouble develops, and then will alert the community service agency to replace the failed circuit.

Through an environmental control system, the computer will analyze the air for impurities, odor, temperature, and moisture content. The air will be filtered, warmed or cooled, moisture added or removed, and a pleasant odor injected — all directed by the computer.

The computer will keep health records of all family members and will prescribe the type and amount of exercise needed. Each morning, a "medicouch" will record an individual's blood pressure, pulse rate, temperature, and weight and will take an electrocardiogram. This information will be fed into the computer.

Based on each person's nutritional needs, the computer will suggest daily menus and will keep an inventory of foodstuffs. The person responsible for meals will push buttons on the kitchen console to select meals to be served at a chosen time.

The kitchen will contain a food processor that is both a freezer and microwave oven. The various portions will be fed automatically from the freezer into the oven for a few seconds of thawing or warming. A dishmaker that uses powdered plastic will produce disposable dishware quickly and cheaply, eliminating dishwashing and dish storage.

Electronics will be used for shopping, too. The console will be equipped with a video screen that will put individuals in fingertip contact via microwave transmission with the store of their choice.

As the video shopper scans shelves and counters, the person at home will order by pushbutton. The store computer will total the bill and will send the amount to the home computer and to the computer in the family's bank. The bank computer will automatically adjust the balances at the bank and in the home.

There will also be a console to give an up-to-the-minute report on the bank balance, the amount owed in taxes, or other financial information.

Information will be available through a machine that transmits and receives electronically all types of written material, including mail, and that delivers news and stock-market reports. It will be possible to check weather conditions throughout the country by means of satellites.

The education room will contain a variety of devices designed to satisfy the learning needs of all members of the family.

The audio center will provide taped instruction in foreign languages, mathematics, space navigation, or whatever subjects are desired. Another area, called the library terminal, will specialize in computer-assisted instruction. Equipment will be programmed with courses ranging from the most elementary reading instructions to the most complicated science course.

The library terminal will tap the home computer for answers that might be found in the encyclopedia. It also may draw from a community library computer that stores more exhaustive information on all disciplines.

Students will be supplied daily with a reel

This video screen in the Philco-Ford "House of Tomorrow" is designed for shopping from home. (Courtesy Philco-Ford Corporation)

of tape instead of books. This tape will provide all video and audio materials for home study and will reproduce enlarged copies of maps and pictures from the home computer and central library facility.

Television and a huge TV screen will be the dominant feature of living areas of A.D. 1999. The TV screen will be holographic, or three-dimensional.

A console will control light intensity and color to match the entertainment mood of the moment.

The use of leisure time is an important consideration in designing the House of Tomorrow. For example, the hobby area will contain highly complex instruments that will take the householder from design to finished product in any medium he cares to work with — clay, glass, wood, metal, or plastic.

An electronic workbench will reproduce patterns that have been fed into the computer for instant recall. In the metal or woodworking area, only one tool will be required, a laser device that will produce a coherent beam of light to cut, drill, and finish materials.

Electronic games will be a feature of the recreation area. A computerized console will enable individuals to play any game in existence, or to invent one. It will even be possible to play checkers with a friend and have the moves recorded on a large TV screen, or to play against the computer if preferred.

Music will be provided electronically. An autocomposer will reproduce the sounds of all instruments, separately or in unison. Original music, or works of the masters that are stored in its electronic memory, will be possible with the aid of the computer.

Such an electronically controlled home that can be programmed to monitor individual

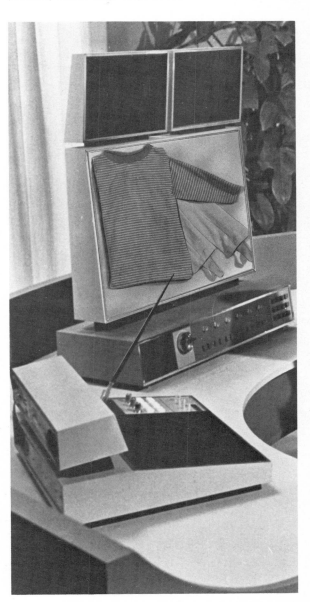

This video screen in the Philco-Ford "House of Tomorrow" is designed for shopping from home. (Courtesy Philco-Ford Corporation)

This is an artist's concept of the Philco-Ford "House of Tomorrow" which has been designed as a prototype for living in the year 1999 A.D.
The dome on the roof at the left is a microwave antenna through which all communications are established with the outside world.
(Courtesy of Philco-Ford Corporation)

The home console in the "House of Tomorrow" will receive information about the bank balance, check weather conditions, scan the news. (Courtesy Philco-Ford Corporation)

The food preparation area includes in the left foreground, a control console for the household computer. In the center is the dishmaker, which uses powdered plastic to make color-keyed disposable dishware quickly and inexpensively. The beverage dispenser (right) makes instantly available hot and cold beverages mixed in quantities controlled by the computer, and the area in right foreground is where creative cooking can be done to supplement meals from the computer. (Courtesy Philco-Ford Corporation)

human needs as well as the details of the day to day operations of a home can be an important asset in providing an environment for the development of human potential.

The rapidly advancing technology of today is opening many new vistas to mankind. Some people are suspicious of this technology—fearful that it is dehumanizing individuals and society. And for some, it may well be. But technology can be a positive force in encouraging people to focus on the human needs of individuals and society if man assumes the full responsibility to use it as a tool for *good* rather than as a scapegoat for his problems.

The many alternatives that are now open and those that will be created each coming year will require thoughtful decisions.

Even today, on the threshold of all this technology, provocative questions come to mind:
Can man learn to harness technology successfully to carry out day-to-day tasks so that he can free his mind to think in relevant terms about major problems of society?
If some of the activities now carried on in the home fulfill psychological and sociological needs of individuals, as well as their physical needs, how will these needs be met when technology takes over the task?
Can home become a true environment for helping individuals reach self-actualization, or will technology make it a place for the fulfillment of bodily needs only?
Will people learn to live with the impersonality of the computer without becoming impersonal themselves?
Can individuals learn to express their individualities in the midst of mass production?
Can individuals understand themselves and

their psychological and sociological needs well enough to embrace the life-style best for them?

This last question is the most important question of all, because how one lives influences so much the human being one becomes.

No one can control his life-style completely. Internal forces such as values, emotions, physical needs, traditions, culture, and goals influence it to a degree. So, too, do external forces such as the community and neighborhood in which one lives, the type of work and work hours, the transportation and shopping facilities for daily living, the individual family situation, and responsibilities. It is possible, however, to gain insight into one's life-style and to make conscious decisions about its direction.

Think about your own daily life-style:
How many of the daily decisions you make are the same ones day after day?
How many could really be changed if a deliberate attempt were made to do so? How would your life-style be changed if you constantly changed a decision about one of the factors?
How would you feel about changing some of these decisions?
To what extent does your home environment influence your life-style? Are there some things about it you would like to change? What is preventing you from making these changes?

The larger philosophic questions also shape a life-style: how one feels about life, about man's responsibility to man, about self, about an omnipotent power, and about the future. These are the very questions that are being challenged by the many new alternatives that changing family patterns and new technology present.

To make a deliberate decision about what life-style will be embraced in the midst of all this change is not an easy task. It demands an understanding of individual human needs as well as a considerable degree of maturity, and a good measure of soul searching. This kind of thinking is an important prelude to planning a home environment to which people can relate. Today's home must be people centered rather than furnishings centered.

Benjamim Disraeli declared the importance of home with these words: "The best security for civilization is the dwelling, and upon proper and becoming dwellings depends more than anything else the improvement of mankind."

Winston Churchill said it another way: "We shape our buildings and then they shape us."

"The history of man is written in the habitations he has wrested from nature. Each civilization has left us, as the main statement of it values, the edifices man erected to house himself or honor his gods.

The characteristic that will mark 20th-century man, and particularly the American of this century, is the persistence with which he struggles to create a fitting habitation for his own personal life and for that of his family. The opposite of materialistic (as some critics claim), this urge to create a fitting and significant habitation for daily life surely reflects the feeling that man is the most important thing in life. For when man is housed so that he can grow and develop the creative soul within him, each generation surpasses the last and the whole human race is moved toward divinity."

This is the ultimate and most noble purpose of furnishing homes for people, for only as individuals grow and develop to their fullest potential can they manage the challenge of a changing society.

SOURCES OF INFORMATION

Challenge of the 70's, a presentation by Joseph Carriero, Chairman, Department of Design and Environmental Analysis, New York State College of Human Ecology, Cornell University to Illinois Chapter, National Home Fashions League.

Cooper, David, *The Death of the Family*, Pantham Press, New York, 1972.

Craig, Nancy, "Cuisine 80," *House Beautiful*, February 1971.

Home Furnishings Daily, April 11, 1967.

"Man's Perpetual pursuit: Shaping His World into a Proper Habitation," *House Beautiful*, April 1960.

"The American Family," *Look*, January 26, 1971.

"Can You Choose a Life Style?" *Penney's Forum*, Fall and Winter 1971.

Philco-Ford Corporation, Philadelphia, Pennsylvania.

"The American Family: Future Uncertain," *Time*, December 28, 1970, pp. 34–39.

Whirlpool Corporation, Benton Harbor, Michigan.

Index